Ranger Rick's NatureScope

TREES ARE TERRIFIC!

National Wildlife Federation

LEARNING TRIANGLE PRESS

*Connecting
kids, parents, and teachers
through learning*

An imprint of McGraw-Hill

New York San Francisco Washington, D.C. Auckland Bogotá Caracas
Lisbon London Madrid Mexico City Milan Montreal New Delhi
San Juan Singapore Sydney Tokyo Toronto

Library of Congress Cataloging-in-Publication Data

Trees are terrific!/National Wildlife Federation.
     p. cm.—(Ranger Rick's Naturescope)
  Includes bibliographical references (p. 94) and index.
  ISBN 0-07-047101-0 (pbk.)
  1. Trees—Study and teaching (Elementary)—Activity programs.
  2. Forest ecology—Study and teaching (Elementary)—Activity programs.
  I. National Wildlife Federation. II. Series.
  QK476.T74 1998
  372.3' 57—dc21   97-36212
                                 CIP

McGraw-Hill

A Division of The *McGraw·Hill* Companies

NATIONAL WILDLIFE FEDERATION®

  2 3 4 5 6 7 8 9 JDL/JDL 9 0 3 2 1 0 9 8

ISBN 0-07-047101-0

NatureScope® was originally conceived by National Wildlife Federation's School Programs Editorial Staff, under the direction of Judy Braus, Editor. Special thanks to all of the Editorial Staff, Scientific, Educational Consultants and Contributors who brought this series of eighteen publications to life.

NATIONAL WILDLIFE FEDERATION EDITORIAL STAFF
Creative Services Manager: Sharon Schiliro
Editor, Ranger Rick® magazine: Gerry Bishop
Director, Classroom-related Programs: Margaret Tunstall
Contributors: Carol J. Boggis, Joan Gould, Heather Karlson

McGRAW-HILL EDP STAFF
Acquisitions Editor: Judith Terrill-Breuer
Editorial Supervisor: Patricia V. Amoroso
Production Supervisor: Claire Stanley
Designer: York Production Services
Cover Design: David Saylor
Contributing Editor: Carol J. Boggis

RRNS

OTHER TITLES IN *RANGER RICK'S NATURESCOPE*

GOAL

Ranger Rick's NatureScope is a creative education series dedicated to inspiring in children an understanding and appreciation of the natural world while developing the skills they will need to make responsible decisions about the environment.

WE ALL NEED TREES

GOAL

Ranger Rick's NatureScope is a creative education series dedicated to inspiring in children an understanding and appreciation of the natural world while developing the skills they will need to make responsible decisions about the environment.

Trees really deserve a lot of respect. They provide homes and food for wildlife, help prevent soil erosion, and even act as "water filters" in many natural communities. They are also a big part of people's lives—in more ways than most of us realize. (Take a look at "From Paper to Plastic" on page 65 for some examples of the many ways we use trees.)

In *Trees Are Terrific!* we've got a lot of tree teaching ideas for you—ideas that you can use throughout the year. We've also provided some ways you and your group can "show your gratitude" to trees, such as by planting trees, taking care of neglected city trees, and raising money to support groups that are working to protect trees and forests around the world.

So have fun teaching your group about trees. And be sure to let your kids know how important it is to be *nice* to trees!

Judy Braus

"So! . . . The little sweethearts were going to carve their initials on me, eh?"

(Reprinted by permission of Chronicle Features of San Francisco)

NatureScope is published by the National Wildlife Federation, 1400 16th St. NW, Washington, DC 20036-2266.
Copyright 1985, 1989, 1992 by the National Wildlife Federation. All rights reserved.
Permission is granted, without written request, to copy pages specified as "Copycat Pages," as well as those sections of the text specifically designated for student use. The reproduction of any other pages of this book is strictly prohibited without written permission from the publisher, the National Wildlife Federation.

Editor: Judy Braus
Associate Editor: Jody Marshall
Assistant Editors: Cindy Van Cleef, Luise Woelflein, Bruce Norfleet, and Carol Hindes
Designer: Kim Kerin
Illustrators: Tina B. Isom, Kim Kerin, and Jack Shepherd
Production Editors: Robyn Gregg and Cindy Van Cleef
Editorial Assistant: Rhonda Lucas
Art Assistant: Jack Shepherd
Development Assistant: Meryl L. Hall
Contributors: Michael Caduto, S. Douglas Miller, and Douglas Weeks
Editorial Consultants: E. Gerald Bishop and Claire Miller

Scientific and Educational Consultants: John E. Hench, Wildlife Biologist, Maryland-National Capital Park and Planning Commission, Silver Spring, Maryland; Dr. Ron Howard, Department of 4-H Youth, Purdue University, West Lafayette, Indiana; Dr. Edward Kurtz, Department of Life Sciences, University of Texas of the Permian Basin, Odessa, Texas; Grace Lieberman, Education Specialist, World Wildlife Fund U.S., Washington, DC; Dr. Terry L. Sharik, Department of Biology, Virginia Tech, Blacksburg, Virginia; Dr. W. Shropshire, Smithsonian Environmental Research Center, Rockville, Maryland; and Andy Stahl, Northwest Natural Resources Center, National Wildlife Federation, Portland, Oregon.

Special thanks to Kathy McGlauflin, Director of *Project Learning Tree,* and Carlton Owen, Director of Allied Audience Programs, American Forest Institute, Washington, DC.

A Close-Up Look At Trees Are Terrific!

L ooking at the Table of Contents, you can see we've divided *Trees Are Terrific!* into five main chapters, each dealing with a broad tree theme, followed by a craft section and the Appendix.

Each of the five chapters includes *background information* that explains concepts and vocabulary, *activities* that relate to the chapter theme, and *Copycat Pages* that reinforce many of the concepts in the activities.

You can choose single activity ideas or teach each chapter as a unit. Either way, each activity stands by itself and includes teaching objectives, materials needed, suggested age groups, subjects covered, and a step-by-step explanation of how to do the activity. (The objectives, materials, age groups, and subjects are highlighted in the left-hand margin for easy reference.)

Age Groups

The suggested age groups are:
- Primary (grades K-2)
- Intermediate (grades 3-5)
- Advanced (grades 6-8)

Each chapter usually begins with primary activities and ends with intermediate or advanced activities. But don't feel bound by the grade levels we suggest. You'll be able to adapt many of these activities to fit your particular age group and needs.

Outdoor Activities

Even if you don't live in a forested area, there are many tree-related activities you can do outside. We've tried to include at least one outdoor activity in each chapter. These are coded in the chapters in which they appear with this symbol:

Copycat Pages

The *Copycat Pages* supplement the activities and include ready-to-copy games, puzzles, coloring pages, and worksheets. *Answers to Copycat Pages are on the inside back cover or in the text of the activity.*

What's At The End

The sixth section, *Crafty Corner,* will give you some art and craft ideas that complement many of the activities in the first five chapters. And the last section, the *Appendix,* is loaded with reference suggestions that include books, films, and tree posters. The *Appendix* also has tree questions and answers, a tree glossary, and suggestions for where to get more tree information.

TABLE OF CONTENTS

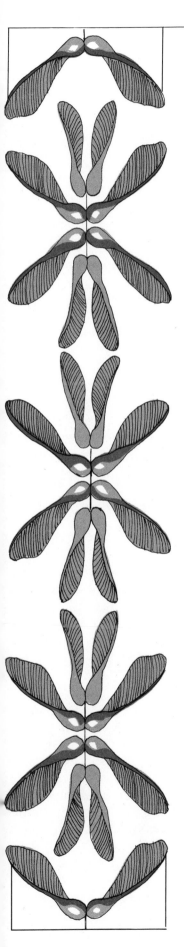

WHAT MAKES A TREE A TREE?

veryone knows what a tree is. Right? Trees are those tall green things with leafy branches that grow along sidewalks, line city parks, and stand side by side in forests. But wait. Not all trees are tall. Some Arctic spruces, for example, never grow more than a foot (.3 m) tall. And not all trees have leafy branches either. Saguaro cactuses, which are a type of tree, have spines instead of leaves.

SO WHAT IS A TREE?

It's harder to define what a tree is than you might think. Although trees share similar characteristics, there are always exceptions that don't fit a nice, neat definition. But here are some of the main ways that trees differ from other types of plants:

Super-sized Plants: Although there are exceptions, most trees grow much taller than other kinds of plants. For example, you'll never run into a 100-foot (30-m) dandelion. But 100-foot (30-m) trees are very common. Unlike most other plants, trees have woody roots, trunks, and limbs that provide the physical support that allows them to grow so tall (see page 6).

Some scientists use size as a way to help define trees. They say that trees are plants that are 15 to 25 feet (5 to 8 m) tall and have a stem (trunk) that is at least 3 to 4 inches (8 to 10 cm) thick. But many scientists don't include a height or diameter limit since trees that grow in very harsh environments, such as Arctic spruces, are often much smaller than other plants.

Redwood trees in the Pacific Northwest are the tallest living organisms. They can grow more than 350 feet (105 m) tall.

A Trunk That Stands on Its Own Roots: Trees are not only taller than most plants, they are also built in a special way. Most trees have one main woody trunk that supports the entire tree. This makes them different from shrubs or vines. (Shrubs often have many woody stems. Vines often have a woody stem, but the stem can't support the weight of the plant.)

Growing Old Gracefully: Trees live longer than most other plants. In fact, some of the oldest living things on earth are trees. For example, bristlecone pines can live for over 4500 years!

Unlike *annuals* (plants that sprout, reproduce, and die in one season) and *biennials* (plants that sprout, reproduce, and die in two seasons), trees are a type of *perennial*. Perennials live for many seasons. Non-woody perennials, such as lilies and irises, die back each year and pass through the dormant season as underground roots, stems, bulbs, or tubers. But trees don't die back. Many do become dormant during the winter, but the stems, branches, and twigs (as well as the roots) are still alive and will continue to grow taller and thicker each year. And because of their unique "plumbing" (see page 6) and their strong, woody support system, trees can survive much longer than other perennials.

KINDS OF TREES

Trees come in different shapes and sizes, from gnarled old bristlecone pines to prickly saguaro cactuses. Worldwide, there are over 20,000 different species of trees. Over 800 grow in North America.

Trees are classified according to how they reproduce, what types of flowers and seeds they have (if any), how they grow, and how they are structured inside. (Sometimes trees that look very much alike are not closely related.) Most trees fall into these two main plant groups:

Gymnosperms (JIM-no-sperms): Plants that have "naked" seeds, which means the seeds are not enclosed in flowers (and later, fruit). (Gymnosperms do not produce true flowers or fruit.) In most gymnosperms, the seeds are produced on the surface of the scales of female cones. Most gymnosperms are pollinated by the wind.

Conifers are the most common types of gymnosperms. Pines, hemlocks, redwoods, spruces, and firs are all types of conifers. Coniferous trees are also called needle-leaved trees because most have thin, needlelike leaves. There are about 500 species of conifers in the world.

Angiosperms (AN-gee-oh-sperms): Flowering plants. Angiosperms are the only types of plants that have true flowers and bear their seeds in fruits. There are over 235,000 species of angiosperms. Oaks, willows, maples, birches, palms, and all other broad-leaved trees (trees with flat, broad leaves) are in this plant group. So are all the flowering non-trees, such as tulips, blackberries, poppies, and so on.

Note: Some scientists also consider tree ferns to be a type of tree. Tree ferns belong to the fern plant group. The members of this group do not produce seeds, flowers, or fruit. Instead they reproduce by spores. Although some tree ferns get to be over 80 feet (24 m) tall and live for many years, they don't have the same woody structure that most other trees have.

TONS OF TREE TERMS

There are all kinds of general tree terms floating around that can make learning about trees pretty confusing. We've already talked about needle-leaved trees and broad-leaved trees. Here are a few more tree terms that you'll often see:

Hardwoods: Foresters often call broad-leaved trees "hardwoods" because most broad-leaved trees have harder wood than do needle-leaved trees. For example, maples and oaks are known for their tough, hard wood and are often used to make high-quality furniture and floors. But the term hardwood is confusing because some broad-leaved trees, such as cottonwoods and magnolias, have very soft, lightweight wood.

Softwoods: Softwood is another confusing term because not all softwoods are soft. Foresters use the term softwood to describe needle-leaved trees, such as pines, spruces, and redwoods, because most have softer wood than do broad-leaved trees. But some softwoods, such as yellow pines and yews, have very hard wood.

Deciduous and Evergreen Trees: Deciduous trees are trees that lose all of their leaves every year. (In temperate regions most lose their leaves in fall.) Evergreen trees do not lose all their leaves at once. Instead they go through a gradual replacement. Each year they produce some new leaves, but, unlike deciduous trees, they drop only the oldest ones each year. (Most evergreen leaves stay on a tree from 2 to 4 years before dropping.) So instead of being bare in winter, as deciduous trees are in many areas, evergreen trees have leaves year round.

In North America, almost all broad-leaved trees are deciduous, but a few are not. For example, holly trees, live oaks, and palms are broad-leaved trees that do not drop their leaves in fall. (In the tropics, however, most broad-leaved trees don't drop their leaves during one season. Instead they lose their leaves gradually and remain green all year.) Most needle-leaved trees in North America are evergreen. But a few needle-leaved trees, such as larches, are deciduous.

TREE PARTS AND HOW THEY "WORK"

Although there are thousands of different kinds of trees in the world, most trees work in much the same way. Here's a look at how the parts of a tree work together to help a tree get the food, water, and minerals it needs to survive.

The Trunk: The trunk of a tree is important for two reasons: First, it acts as a support rod, giving the tree its shape and strength. Second, it acts as the central "plumbing system" in a tree, forming a network of tubes that carries water and minerals up from the roots to the leaves, and food (sugar) from the leaves down to the branches, trunk, and roots.

The easiest way to see how a tree works is to look at a cross section of the trunk. Here are the five main layers you would see, and what each layer does (see the diagram on page 10):

1. Barking Up the Right Tree: The outer layer of the trunk (and branches) is called the *outer bark* or just the *bark*. Tree bark can be smooth, scaly, rubbery, flaky, craggy, or bumpy. Its texture, thickness, and flexibility depend on the type of tree. Although bark looks different from tree to tree, it serves the same purpose—to protect the tree from injury and disease. Some trees have very thick bark that helps prevent damage from fires. Others have bad-tasting chemicals in their bark that discourage hungry insects. And some bark is covered with spines or thorns that keep browsing mammals away.

The bark of large Douglas firs and sequoias may be more than two feet (.6 m) thick.

2. Food Is for Phloem: The layer next to the outer bark is called the *inner bark* or *phloem* (FLOW-um). The phloem is a thin layer that acts as a food supply line from the leaves to the rest of the tree. Sap (water containing dissolved sugars and nutrients) travels down from the leaves through channels in the phloem to the branches, trunk, and roots, supplying all the living parts of the tree with food. At certain times during the year, the phloem also transports stored sugars up from the roots to the rest of the tree. (If you were to cut a band around the trunk, through the bark and phloem, the tree would probably die. That's because the phloem would be severed and food could no longer flow to the lower trunk and roots.)

3. Keep 'em Coming, Cambium: Next to the phloem is a very thin layer called the *cambium*. (It is often only one or two cells thick, and you need a microscope to see it well.) The cambium is one of the growing layers of the tree, making new cells during the growing season that become part of the phloem, part of the xylem (see below), or more cambium. The cambium is what makes the trunk, branches, and roots grow thicker.

4. Up, Up, and Away with Sapwood: The layer next to the cambium is called the *sapwood* or *new xylem*. The sapwood is made up of the youngest layers of wood. (Each year the cambium adds new layers of woody tissue.) The sapwood is a network of thick-walled cells that forms a pipeline, carrying water and minerals up the tree from the roots to the leaves and other parts of the tree. The sapwood also stores nutrients and transports them across the tree, from one part to another.

5. A Dead Heart: Most of the trunk in an old tree is dead wood called *heartwood* or just plain *wood*. The heartwood is *old xylem* that no longer transports water and minerals up the tree. (After a few years the sapwood in most trees gets filled in with resinlike material and slowly changes into heartwood. The new xylem is the only part of the wood that works as a transport system.) The heartwood is often much darker in color than the sapwood.

The heartwood gives the tree support. But sometimes it rots away, leaving a hollow, living tree. Hollow trees often topple over or split apart in storms because they are very weak after the heartwood has decayed.

Note: Palm trees have a different type of structure than most other trees. They do not have real branches and produce no annual rings. (See page 16 for more about rings.) Instead they grow taller without growing thicker.

The Roots: A tree's roots are long, underground branches that spread out to help anchor the tree and to absorb water and nutrients from the soil. Some trees have long taproots that reach straight down for 15 feet (4.5 m) or more. Other trees have more shallow root systems that lie closer to the surface of the ground.

Large taproots and lateral roots branch into smaller and smaller roots. An average tree has millions of these small rootlets, each covered with thousands of fine *root hairs*. The root hairs make it easier to soak up water and dissolved minerals from the soil. (Most of the rootlets lie very close to the surface of the ground where most of the water and nutrients are located.)

The Leaves: From skinny pine needles to broad palm leaves, all tree leaves serve the same purpose—to make food for the tree. Leaves use carbon dioxide from the air, water from the roots, and the sun's energy (in the form of sunlight), to make sugar (glucose). This food-making chemical reaction is called *photosynthesis*. Photosynthesis can take place only in the presence of *chlorophyll*—the green pigment that is found in all green plants. Chlorophyll absorbs the sunlight needed for photosynthesis. During photosynthesis the leaves release oxygen which becomes part of the air that we and other animals breathe.

Water and Trees: Trees, like all living things, could not survive without water. Here are some of the reasons that water is so important to a tree:
- a large percentage of each living cell in a tree is made up of water
- water helps move dissolved minerals and gases from cell to cell
- water pressure inside a leaf's cells helps maintain the leaf's shape
- water is needed in order for photosynthesis to occur (Water for photosynthesis is carried up through the xylem network from the roots.)
- water carries dissolved sugars (made during photosynthesis) down through the network of phloem to the branches, trunk, and roots

Although trees use a lot of water every day, they also lose a lot of water. About 99% of the water the roots absorb from the soil evaporates from the leaves through a process called *transpiration*. (Water evaporates through tiny pores in the leaf [stomata] as carbon dioxide—also needed for photosynthesis—rushes in. During photosynthesis there is a trade-off between water loss and carbon dioxide gain.) As water evaporates, it pulls up more water from the roots to the leaf. This "transpiration pull" is one of the things that help move water and minerals through the tree and help keep trees cool in hot weather.

Oxygen for Energy: Like almost all living cells, tree cells need oxygen in order to break down the sugar (or starch) and release the energy they need to grow. The cells in the leaves, trunk, branches, and twigs absorb oxygen from the air. The cells in the roots absorb oxygen from the soil. (Without oxygen, tree cells would die. That's why many trees drown if their roots become waterlogged.)

Leaf It to Us!

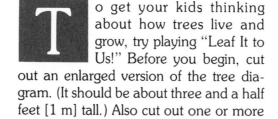

To get your kids thinking about how trees live and grow, try playing "Leaf It to Us!" Before you begin, cut out an enlarged version of the tree diagram. (It should be about three and a half feet [1 m] tall.) Also cut out one or more construction paper leaves for everyone.

Tape or hang the paper tree on the wall (at a height all the children can reach) and stick a circle of tape to each branch tip. Put the leaves in a pile near the tree, set up the music, and you're ready to play the game. Here's what to do:

Have the kids sit in a semicircle around the tree. Explain that everyone will get to help "dress up" the paper tree with the cutout leaves. But before a player can put a leaf on the tree, he or she must answer a tree question.

Next give one of the children a beanbag. Start the music, and have the kids pass the beanbag around the semicircle. When the music stops, ask whoever ends up with the beanbag one of the questions below. After a player has answered a question correctly, he or she can take one of the leaves from the leaf pile and stick it to one of the tree's branch tips. (If someone gives a wrong answer at first, talk about the question until he or she comes up with the right answer. That way everyone who answers a question will be able to put a leaf on the tree, even if the original answer isn't right.)

Continue playing until all of the leaves are on the tree, making sure everyone gets to answer at least one question. (You may need to add a few questions to our list, depending on the size of your group.) To follow up, you might want to take the kids outside to look at some real trees. (See "Tree Tots" on page 9.)

QUESTIONS

1. Hold up a "non-tree" object such as a rock and ask, "Is this part of a tree?"
2. What happens to some tree leaves in the fall? (On some trees [most deciduous trees], the leaves turn different colors and fall off in one season. On most pines and other evergreens they don't change colors and they don't all fall off during one season.)
3. Can you think of a way a bird might use a tree? (Many birds perch in trees, build nests in trees, and/or roost [sleep or rest] in trees. Also, some birds eat a tree's fruit or nuts or eat the insects that live in or on trees.)
4. Can you think of a way a tree's bark can help the tree? (Bark protects a tree from certain insects, cold weather, and other things that could harm it.)
5. Hold up a pine cone and ask, "What is this?"
6. Can you name a kind of food that people get from trees? (apples, oranges, cherries, and other fruits; also walnuts, pecans, and many other nuts)
7. Can you name a kind of animal that lives in trees? (Many bats, birds, insects, spiders, squirrels, and other animals often live in trees.)
8. Is a tree a living thing?
9. Is a tree a plant or an animal?
10. Hold up some pine needles and ask, "What are these?"
11. What do a tree's roots do? (They absorb water and minerals and help hold the tree steady in the soil.)
12. What is a big group of trees all living in the same place called? (a woods or forest)
13. Can you name something made from trees that people use every day? (Paper, pencils, and wooden furniture are just a few examples.)
14. When there are no leaves on a tree in winter, does that necessarily mean the tree is dead? (No. Trees that lose their leaves in fall stay alive all through the winter in a kind of resting stage.)
15. Would trees be able to grow if the earth never got any sunshine? (No. Trees, like most plants, need sunshine to grow.)
16. What color are most trees' leaves most of the time? (green)
17. Can you name a color some leaves become in the fall? (Yellow, red, orange, purple, brown. The leaves of some trees stay green all year.)
18. When you grow up, will you be taller or shorter than most kinds of trees get to be when they're old? (shorter)
19. Can you name a way an insect might use a tree? (Some insects eat tree leaves, bark, seeds, and other tree parts; some insects lay their eggs on or in trees; some katydids and other insects "sing" from perches in trees.)

20. If there were tall trees all around your house, would you feel warmer or cooler in the house on a hot summer day? (cooler)

21. Hold up a piece of bark and ask, "Is this part of a tree?" (Also ask where bark is found on a tree [on the trunk, branches, and roots].)

22. If you lived in a place that was windy all the time and you planted some big pine trees around your house, would as much wind blow against your house as it did before the trees were planted? (No. Trees make good windbreaks.)

23. Hold up an orange and ask, "Is this part of a tree?" (An orange is the fruit of an orange tree.)

24. Hold up an acorn and ask, "What would this grow into if it were planted?" (an oak tree)

Tree Tots

Talk about the parts of a tree and take a tree walk.

Objectives:
Name some of the parts of a tree. Talk about how these parts help trees.

Ages:
Primary

Materials:
- *leaves from several different kinds of trees*
- *twigs, bark, fruit, nuts, or other tree parts*
- *pictures of trees and tree parts*
- *paper*
- *construction paper*
- *tape*
- *marker (optional)*
- *glue (optional)*
- *yarn (optional)*

Subject:
Science

Here's an activity that will help younger children look more closely at trees. First they'll learn about some of the different "parts" that make up a tree, and afterward you can take them on a walk outside to compare some of the different trees in your area.

Before the kids arrive, find four or five different kinds of trees around your school or nature center and collect some leaves from each one. (Collect a leaf for each child in your group. If you gather the leaves quite a while before you do the activity, you can keep them fresh by wrapping them in a wet towel.) Also collect a few twigs, pieces of bark, and other tree parts. Keep in mind where all of the trees are located so you can find them again when you take the kids for a walk.

Once you're back inside, trace an outline of each kind of leaf on a piece of paper. (You may need to enlarge the outlines and go over them with a dark marker so they'll be easy to see from a distance.) Tape or hang each of the leaf outlines in a different place in the room.

When you're ready to start the activity, have the kids sit in a circle. Then lead a discussion about the different parts of a tree, showing them pictures of leaves, bark, branches, roots, and other tree parts as you talk. Pass around any parts you collected before the activity. You may also want to talk about what each tree part does. (See the background information on pages 6 and 7.)

After the discussion, give each child one of the leaves you collected. To help them observe their leaves closely, ask the kids some questions. For example, are the leaf edges pointed or smooth? Are any of the leaves a different color from the others? Do any of the leaves have tiny hairs on their undersides? Can you see and feel the veins? Also ask the kids if there's anything special about any of their leaves. (For example, some may notice that their leaves have been munched on by insects or other animals.)

Next tell the kids that there's a picture of each type of leaf hanging somewhere in the room. Have them look for the leaf outline that matches their particular leaf, then have each of them go and stand next to the correct picture.

Once all the kids have found the right leaf shape, tell them that they're going to be taking a walk outside to find the trees the leaves came from. (Have them take their leaves with them outside. If you're working with very young kids you may want to have them wear their leaves around their necks. Just glue or tape the leaves to pieces of construction paper and attach enough string or yarn to fit over the kids' heads.)

Explain that each group of kids with the same kind of leaf should keep their eyes peeled for "their" tree. Then stop at certain trees as you walk along and ask if anyone thinks his or her leaf came from that particular tree. Have the kids who say yes hold their leaves up in the air. Next have all of the kids look for some of the tree's parts on the ground. Can any of them find any twigs and buds, fruit or nuts, other leaves, or any other tree "pieces"? Have them compare the parts they find to those of the other trees you stop and talk about.

Build a Tree

Objectives:
Describe the parts of a tree. Explain how each part works.

Ages:
Primary and Intermediate

Materials:
- *slips of paper*
- *chalkboard or easel paper*

Subject:
Science

In this activity, your group can learn about the parts of a tree by acting them out and building a "human tree." Before you begin, copy these words onto separate slips of paper and put them in a hat (you should end up with 30 slips):

- heartwood (1)
- sapwood (2)
- cambium (4)
- phloem (8)
- outer bark (12)
- taproot (1)
- lateral roots (2)

(Adjust the number of slips you make according to the size of your group.)

Next copy the diagram below on the chalkboard or easel paper and label the parts. Then, using the background information on pages 6 and 7, discuss each part with the group, explaining how each functions and where it's located on a tree.

Now take the group outside to a large open area and explain that everyone will work together to "build" a tree. First have each person pick a part to play by reaching into the hat and pulling out a slip of paper. Next have the kids practice any sounds or movements suggested for their parts and then have them slowly build the tree, layer by layer. Once the tree is built, have them act out their parts together.

1. Have the child playing the part of the *heartwood* cross his or her arms and stand in the center of the play area. Explain that this child represents the heartwood of the tree.
2. Next have the child playing the *taproot* sit down at the foot of the heartwood kid. Explain that this person represents the deep taproot that most trees have.
3. Have the *lateral roots* lie down on their backs, spreading out from the taproot with their feet toward the heartwood. (Have the lateral roots make slurping sounds.)
4. Have the *sapwood* kids join hands to make a ring around the heartwood. Position them so they stand between the lateral roots. They should face in, toward the heartwood. (Have the sapwood kids pretend they are drawing water up from the roots by lowering their hands, still joined, and then raising them above their heads.)
5. Have the *cambium* kids join hands and form a large circle around the sapwood. (Have the cambium kids chant, "we make new cells, we make new cells, we make new cells.")

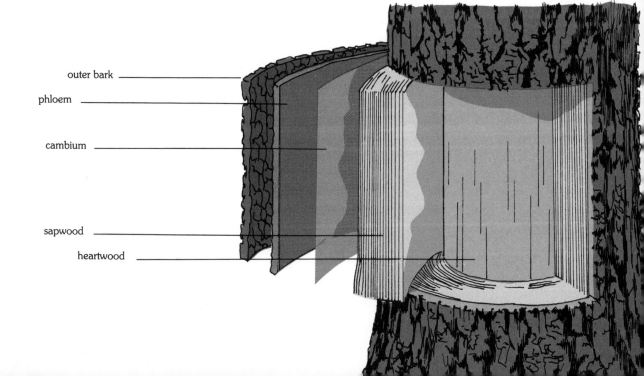

6. Next have the *phloem* kids join hands and form a larger circle around the cambium. (Have the phloem kids pretend they are transporting food down from the leaves by starting out holding their arms above their heads, then lowering them and raising them again.)
7. Finally, have the *outer bark* kids form a circle around the entire tree, facing outward and holding hands.

Once everyone is in position, ask the kids to go through their motions: the roots taking up water from the soil, the sapwood transporting the water up the trunk to the branches and leaves, the phloem carrying food down from the leaves to the trunk and roots, and the cambium chanting "we make new cells." Afterward, lead a short discussion about the different parts of the tree to make sure everyone understands what each part does.

(This idea was adapted with permission from Joseph Cornell, author of *Sharing Nature with Children,* Ananda Publications, Nevada City, California 95959.)

Eat a Leaf

Make a model of a leaf cross section with gelatin and fruit.

Objective:
Describe the structure of a leaf.

Ages:
Intermediate and Advanced

Materials:
* *one or more 8 × 8-inch (20 × 20-cm) glass pans*
* *gelatin (two 6-oz [168-g] packages of yellow gelatin and one 6-oz [168-g] package of green gelatin per pan)*
* *water*
* *heat source*
* *bananas, cantaloupe, grapes, strawberries, or other fruit*
* *whipped cream*
* *large spoon*
* *mixing bowl*
* *refrigerator or freezer*
* *spoons*
* *plates*
* *microscope (optional)*
* *slides of leaf cross sections (optional— see the end of the activity for information on how to order)*
* *drawing paper*
continued next page)

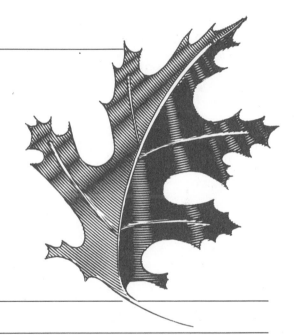

By making gelatin models of leaves, your kids can learn about the layers of a leaf and then eat a tasty snack.

Start the activity by drawing a simple sketch of a leaf cross section onto the chalkboard or a large piece of easel paper. (See next page for reference.) Then pass out paper and colored pencils, crayons, or markers. Use the information below to talk about the different layers of a leaf, and have the kids draw and label their own leaf cross sections during the discussion.

LEAF LINGO

Upper and Lower Epidermis: These two layers make up the protective "skin" of a leaf. They let in light and are usually coated with a waxy covering that reduces water loss. Stomata, which are tiny holes that open and close to let in carbon dioxide and release oxygen, are part of a leaf's epidermal layers. (Most stomata are found in the lower epidermis. A single leaf can have more than a million stomata!)

Mesophyll (also called the *ground layer*): This middle layer of a leaf is made up of several other layers:

The *spongy layer* contains loosely packed, differently shaped cells. Gases that take part in photosynthesis pass into this layer through a leaf's stomata. Some cells in the spongy layer have chloroplasts that contain chlorophyll, the pigment that absorbs light energy to power photosynthesis.

The *palisade layer* contains many chloroplasts in its cells. Most of the reactions in photosynthesis occur in this layer.

The *veins* branch out to almost every cell in a leaf. They bring water and minerals to the leaf cells and carry sugar out of the leaf.

Once you've discussed the layers of a leaf, have the kids make a couple of edible leaf models by following the directions we've provided. Then use the models to review leaf layers. (To give the kids an idea of where each layer in a leaf is located and how all the layers fit together, talk about the gelatin models and the layers represented in them before serving them to the kids. Once the gelatin models are cut, the layers will tend to mix together.)

Point out in the gelatin models the upper and lower epidermal layers (green

- *colored pencils, crayons, or markers*
- *chalkboard or easel paper*

Subject: Science

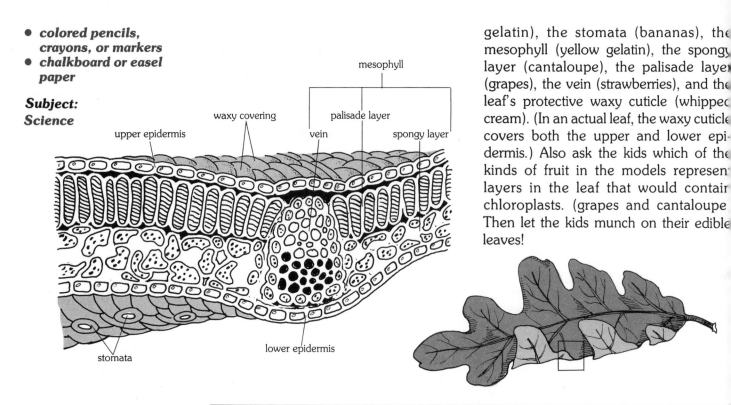

gelatin), the stomata (bananas), the mesophyll (yellow gelatin), the spongy layer (cantaloupe), the palisade layer (grapes), the vein (strawberries), and the leaf's protective waxy cuticle (whipped cream). (In an actual leaf, the waxy cuticle covers both the upper and lower epidermis.) Also ask the kids which of the kinds of fruit in the models represent layers in the leaf that would contain chloroplasts. (grapes and cantaloupe) Then let the kids munch on their edible leaves!

HOW TO MAKE EDIBLE LEAVES

1. For each 8 × 8-inch (20 × 20-cm) glass pan you'll need two packets of yellow gelatin and one packet of green gelatin. You can substitute different types of fruit if the ones we suggest are out of season.

2. Cut a banana into 1/4-inch (6-mm) slices and scatter them over the bottom of the pan.

3. Mix the green gelatin according to the directions on the gelatin box. Before chilling the gelatin, pour just enough of it into the pan to cover the bananas. Save the leftover gelatin and keep it at room temperature.

4. Cool the banana and gelatin mixture in a refrigerator or freezer until the gelatin is firm. (It will take about 1 hour to firm up in a refrigerator and about 30 minutes or less in a freezer.)

5. Make a row of strawberries down the middle of the pan, on top of the gelatin.

6. Scoop out small chunks of cantaloupe and cover the cooled layer with them.

7. Mix the yellow gelatin, then pour it over the strawberries and cantaloupe. Cool the mixture until the yellow layer is firm.

8. Arrange the grapes side by side in rows across the yellow layer.

9. Mix the second package of yellow gelatin and pour it over the grapes, then cool the mixture until this newest layer is firm.

10. Pour the remainder of the green gelatin into the container and cool the mixture one last time.

11. Spread a thin layer of whipped cream over the final layer of green gelatin.

Note: After your group has created and eaten their leafy "food factories," they can take a microscopic look at the cross section of a leaf. You can order slides of leaf cross sections by writing to Carolina Biological Supply at either 2700 York Rd., Burlington, NC, 27215, or at Box 187, Gladstone, OR 97027. Or you can call (800) 334-5551. (You can also check with your local junior or senior high school science department.)

Hidden Colors

Conduct an experiment to separate leaf pigments.

Objective:
Explain how some green leaves turn different colors in the fall.

Ages:
Intermediate and Advanced

Materials:
- green leaves
- nail polish remover
- small glass jars
- coffee filter paper
- pencils
- tape
- scissors
- metal spoons
- rulers
- paper

Subject:
Science

Most green leaves have more color to them than meets the eye. In the spring and summer, they look green because of the pigment called *chlorophyll.* (Chlorophyll absorbs light energy to power photosynthesis.) But there are usually other pigments "hiding" in leaves. We can't see these colors in spring and summer because they're masked by the green color of the chlorophyll. But in the fall, when chlorophyll breaks down, the "hidden" pigments begin to show up. The colors a leaf will become depend on which of these pigments is most prominent. (In some leaves, red pigments don't exist in the leaf during the spring and summer. Instead, they are produced after chlorophyll begins to break down.)

The changing colors of a leaf are a sign that the leaf is dying. Without chlorophyll to power photosynthesis and make food, the leaf soon "starves." Cells in its stem die, and the leaf eventually falls from the branch. (For an explanation of why deciduous trees lose their leaves, see page 26.)

Here's a way for your kids to see some of a leaf's "hidden" colors.
Safety Note: Acetone (nail polish remover) separates the leaf pigments in this experiment. Check to see if your school or organization has any regulations on the use of this chemical. Be sure to keep the room well-ventilated when you use it, and caution the children to avoid breathing the fumes or getting the chemical on their skin or in their eyes. Also, wipe up any spills immediately to keep the acetone from damaging the finish on furniture or floors.

Start the activity by taking the kids outside and dividing the group into pairs. Have each pair collect two or three green leaves. When you come back in, give each pair a pencil, a spoon, a coffee filter, and a glass jar (acetone dissolves Styrofoam or plastic) and have them follow these directions:
1. Tear the green leaves into small pieces and put them into the jar.
2. Add enough nail polish remover to each jar to cover the leaves. (An adult should pour the nail polish remover.)
3. Mash the leaves into a soupy mixture with a spoon and let the mixture stand for five minutes.
4. Cut a 1½-inch (4-cm) by 3½-inch (9-cm) strip from the coffee filter.
5. Tape the filter strip to the pencil (see diagram). Lay the pencil across the top of the jar. Adjust the strip so the end just touches the liquid.

When the liquid has gone about halfway up the strip, have the kids remove their strips and lay them on clean pieces of paper. When the strips are dry have the kids look at the green and yellow bands of color on them. Explain that the acetone in the nail polish remover separated the leaf pigments from the mashed leaf material. When the filter paper soaked up the liquid in the jar it also soaked up the leaf's green and yellow pigments, which traveled different distances up the paper.

Ask the kids what pigment is in the green band of color (chlorophyll). The yellow band comes from a type of pigment called a *carotenoid.* Can anyone say what would happen if the experiment were repeated with leaves that had turned yellow? (Since chlorophyll would have already broken down, only a band of yellow would appear on the filter strip.) Explain to the group that if they tried to separate the pigments in a green leaf that will turn red or purple in the fall, they'd see only green and yellow bands of pigment. One reason for this is that many pigments are made in the fall, after chlorophyll has broken down. Another reason is that some pigments are not separated by acetone.

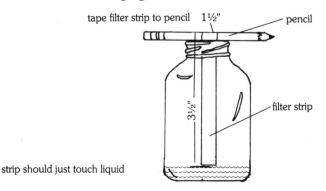

tape filter strip to pencil 1½" pencil
3½"
filter strip
strip should just touch liquid

Keying Out Trees

"Key out" the children in your group, then identify some trees using a simple leaf key.

Objective:
Use a key to identify trees.

Ages:
Intermediate and Advanced

Materials:
- **copies of pages 20, 21, and 22**
- **chalkboard or easel paper**
- **pencils or pens**
- **index cards (optional)**
- **construction paper (optional)**
- **bulletin board (optional)**

Subject:
Science

ow can you figure out the name of a tree you're looking at if you've never seen that kind of tree before? You can use a tree identification key. A tree key is a series of phrases, each of which points out a certain feature of a tree, such as the shape of its leaves, color of its bark, and so on. By determining which phrases apply to your tree, you can identify the tree you are looking at. (There are also keys for wildflowers, birds, shrubs, fish, and many other living things.)

PART 1: "KEYING OUT" KIDS

Using a "people key" is one way to teach your group what a key is and how it works. The tree-shaped diagram on page 20 is a modified key for identifying people. Before you get started using the people key, copy the tree-shaped diagram onto a chalkboard or a large piece of easel paper. (You can also make a more permanent display by sketching the diagram on a bulletin board covered with construction paper.)

Begin the activity by asking the kids how they can tell different people apart. (by their sex, hair color and texture, eye color, height, and other physical features) Why isn't clothing a good way to tell people apart? (because people can change their clothes or wear identical clothes) Then pass out copies of page 20 and have the kids follow along as you explain how the "key" works.

Each of the branches represents a physical feature that helps to tell people apart. By starting at the trunk and moving up the branches that correctly describe the person being "keyed out," you will reach the very tip of an outermost branch. This is the person's position in the key. For example, if you were keying out a blue-eyed girl with straight brown hair and freckles, you would first move up the branch marked "female." At the fork for hair color, you'd climb up the branch for brown hair. After moving up the branch for straight hair and then the branch for blue eyes, you'd finish up at the end of the "freckles" branch. This is where you'd write that person's name. As an example for the kids, try keying out yourself. (This key is designed for an average group of children. If it doesn't fit the individuals in your group, you can adapt the branches already on the tree or add more specific characteristics.)

Now divide the children into pairs. They will work together to key out each other on their diagrams. Carefully looking at their partners, they should go through the key to find each other's position on the key and then write their names at the ends of the branches.

After everyone is finished, have the pairs go up to the large diagram one at a time and fill in their names. (If you're making a bulletin board, the kids can write their names on index cards or leaf-shaped pieces of construction paper, then tape or staple them on the board.)

You may find that several people have been placed at a single position on the key. If this happens, call these children to the front of the room. What other characteristics could identify them? (height, short or long hair, light or dark shade of skin or hair, and so on)

Once everyone's name is on the diagram, go over it as a group. To test the accuracy of your "people key," invite someone into the room who doesn't know the names of the children. Ask one of the children to volunteer, and have the guest "key out" the child to determine his or her name.

Now that they understand how a key works, let your kids try keying out trees by looking at leaves. Give everyone copies of pages 21 and 22. Each of the boxes on page 22 contains a picture of leaves. Explain to the kids that they will identify the type of tree each leaf came from by using the leaf identification key.

Before the kids try to key out the nine leaves, copy the illustrations of the terms found on the bottom of page 21 on the chalkboard or easel paper. Then go over each of the leaf terms with them as they follow along on their papers. (Some children may have trouble with these terms. Before they try keying out the leaves, you may want to go over each of the leaf drawings on page 22, discussing the shape of each leaf and whether it is compound or simple and opposite or alternate.)

Next have the kids look at the dichotomous key on page 21. Explain that the word *dichotomous* comes from two Greek words that, together, mean "to divide into two parts." A dichotomous key is based on the idea of making a choice between two alternatives. As with most keys, each pair of phrases in the leaf key we've provided describes different features. But only one of the phrases correctly describes the leaf being keyed out. As they're keying out their leaves, each person will need to decide which phrase applies to the particular leaf he or she is trying to key out. Explain that this "correct" phrase will either guide the kids to the next pair of phrases or state the name of the tree the leaf grows on.

Now set a time limit and let each of the kids try to key out all nine leaves. As they identify each leaf, they should write the name of the tree it comes from on the line under the drawing.

When the time is up, go over the answers (listed on page 77) with the group.

Tell-Tale Transpiration

Conduct an experiment to demonstrate that trees lose water through transpiration.

Objectives:
Define transpiration. Discuss the movement of water through a tree.

Ages:
Intermediate and Advanced

Materials:
- *leafy branches*
- *several 3-foot (1-m) sections of flexible clear plastic tubing with a diameter of ¼ inch (6 mm)*
- *sharp knife*
- *water*
- *masking tape*
- *waterproof markers*

Subject:
Science

ou can't see it happening, but trees are losing water almost all the time. As stomata (tiny pores) on the surfaces of leaves open and allow carbon dioxide to flow in and oxygen to flow out, water evaporates into the air. This water loss is called *transpiration*.

As a tree transpires, water moves up through the tree and replaces the water that was lost. This moving water transports minerals from the deepest roots to the highest branches. But losing a lot of water can be a problem, so most plants have special adaptations that keep them from transpiring too much. (For more information about some of the ways some plants prevent too much water loss, see pages 15 and 16 of *NatureScope—Discovering Deserts* [Vol. 1, No. 5].)

Your kids can take a close-up look at transpiration by conducting a simple experiment. Divide the kids into groups of three or four and give each group three

cut branch at an angle

feet (1 m) of plastic tubing and a leafy branch from a broad-leaved tree. (You can collect the branches before the kids arrive [and keep the ends in water] or let the kids gather their own. Make sure the ends of the branches can fit into the plastic tubes.) Have each group hold the non-leafy end of their branch under water while you cut off the end at an angle using a sharp knife (see diagram).

(continued next page)

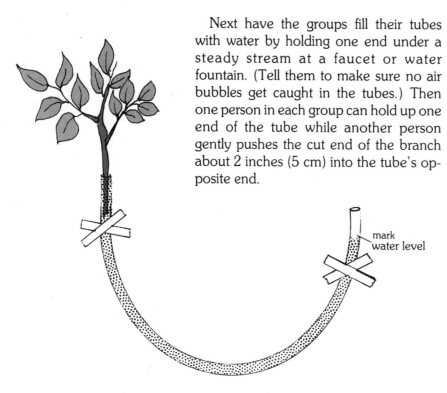

Next have the groups fill their tubes with water by holding one end under a steady stream at a faucet or water fountain. (Tell them to make sure no air bubbles get caught in the tubes.) Then one person in each group can hold up one end of the tube while another person gently pushes the cut end of the branch about 2 inches (5 cm) into the tube's opposite end.

mark
water level

Now tell each group to bend their tubes into a U-shape. Have them use masking tape to attach the tubes to a wall or window in a warm sunny place outside (see diagram). Then have them use a

waterproof marker to mark the water level near the "branchless" end of the tube.

You should also set up a tube without a branch to show that ordinary evaporation is not the only cause of water loss. Seal one end of this control tube with masking tape and leave the other end open. Mark the water level on the open end.

After an hour, let the kids observe the changes in their tubes' water levels. They should be able to see that there is less water in the tubes with leafy branches than there was earlier. The water level in the tube without a branch probably dropped too, but not as much as the others. Explain that water merely evaporated from the "branchless" tube. Some water probably evaporated from the open ends of the tubes with branches—but most of the water loss in these tubes was due to transpiration.

Older kids can test the effects of temperature and sunlight on transpiration by setting up a tube and leafy branch in a warm sunny area and comparing its water loss to that of a similar tube and branch placed in a cool shady spot.

Reading the Rings

Match tree ring patterns with the factors that caused them, then "read" the rings of a tree to solve a mystery.

Objectives:
Describe how events in the life of a tree can affect the growth of its annual rings. Use cross-dating techniques to find out how old a tree is.

Ages:
Advanced

Materials:
● *copies of pages 23 and 24*
● *chalkboard or easel paper*
● *pencils*
● *scissors*

(continued next page)

One of the best ways to learn about how trees grow is to take a close-up look at their annual growth rings. Not only do tree rings tell how old a tree is, they also show what the climatic conditions were like in past years. In this activity your group can find out how to "read" the rings of a tree and then see how scientists use these growth rings to help learn about past climates.

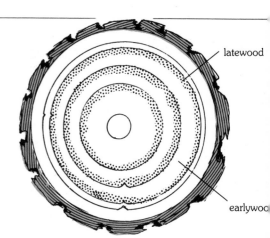

latewood

earlywoo

PART 1: READING THE RINGS

Copy the cross-section illustration above on the chalkboard or on a large piece of easel paper. Using the background information on page 17, explain how annual rings form. If possible, show the kids what the rings look like in a real tree cross section. Try bringing in (or have the kids bring in) a couple of fireplace logs. (You might want to saw the logs into thin

cross sections so each person can have one to look at. The logs can be small and still have clearly defined rings.)

Next pass out copies of page 23 and have everyone look at the cross sections on the left-hand side of the page. Explain that each cross section represents a different tree. On the right-hand side are pictures showing seven factors that can affect tree growth. Go over the factors with the children so they understand each one. Then discuss each cross section and the factor or factors that could have influenced its growth pattern. Have the children draw lines from each cross section to the matching factor or factors.

Cross Section A: The uneven growth shown in the rings could have been caused by a fallen tree leaning against the tree (picture 1). The tree grew more on one side than the other, and curved up around the fallen tree. This uneven ring pattern could also belong to a tree growing on a steep slope (picture 6).

Cross Section B: The scarring in this cross section was caused by a forest fire during the tree's sixth growing season (picture 2).

Cross Section C: The mark beginning in year six is all that's left of a branch that died and fell off (picture 7). Eventually the tree's trunk grew around the remains of the branch and covered it. (The branch could also have been broken or cut off.)

Cross Section D: The narrow rings shown in this cross section could have been caused by several factors such as drought (picture 3), heavy insect damage (picture 4), or damage from construction (picture 5). If a tree lost all or most of its leaves because of an insect attack or drought, it would not be able to make food and would grow very little that year. And root damage from the construction of a house or sidewalk too close to the tree would reduce the water and minerals the roots could take up. Ask the children if they can think of other factors that might cause narrow growth rings. (disease, cold winter, a spring frost, transplanting, competition from other trees for sunlight and nutrients, and so on)

THE INSIDE STORY ON RINGS

Here's some background information about how tree rings form and what conditions influence their growth:

What Are Tree Rings? If you look at a cross section of some tree trunks, you'll often see a distinct pattern of rings. Each ring is a layer of wood produced during the tree's growing season. As a tree begins growing in spring, the cambium (see page 6) produces a light-colored band of thin-walled cells called *earlywood*. As growth slows down in the summer, a darker ring of thick-walled cells called *latewood* is formed. Together, the earlywood and latewood form an *annual growth ring*. In most trees growing in temperate and northern climates, one growth ring is usually laid down each year. In the tropics, where the growing season often continues year round, trees may lay down more than one growth ring in one year. (Not all trees have clearly defined rings. For example, many tropical trees have ring patterns that are very hard to read.)

Good Years and Bad Years: The thicknesses and appearances of a tree's annual growth rings often vary from year to year, depending on growing conditions. During a good growing season, a wide ring is laid down. But during a poor growing season (with drought, an extremely long, cold winter, a spring frost, or some other factor hindering growth), the ring will be much narrower, indicating the tree was able to grow very little.

Other factors besides the weather can influence a tree's growth, including insect damage, diseases (viruses, bacteria, or fungi), fire, root damage, transplanting, and competition from other trees for sunlight, water, or nutrients. (See page 23 for the ways some of these factors influence how tree rings look.) Many things that cause a tree to be "stressed" will eventually show up in its growth ring pattern. If this stress occurs after the growing season, a narrow growth ring will probably be laid down in the next year's growth.

(continued next page)

PART 2: CROSS-DATING DETECTIVES

Scientists have found that they can learn about past climates by studying the ring patterns of very old trees. The science of studying the past by looking at tree rings is called *dendrochronology*.

One way scientists study past climates is by looking at the growth rings of trees which are very sensitive to climatic changes. For example, bristlecone pines are very long-lived trees that grow in areas with very little rainfall. Their growth rings

Luise Woelflein

reflect years of little rain (narrow bands) and years of heavy rain (wide bands) in a way that allows scientists to piece together information about rainfall during past centuries. (Annual growth rings in bristlecone pines are also affected by other climatic conditions, such as temperature, but rainfall is the primary variable.)

Cross dating is another important technique used by dendrochronologists. Cross dating compares the growth rings from one tree to the growth rings of another tree and matches the ring patterns of the years when the two trees both lived.

Scientists use a technique called *coring* to take a look at the rings of a living tree without cutting it down. By drilling into the center of a tree trunk with a special instrument called an *increment borer,* they can remove a piece of wood that is about the thickness of a soda straw. The growth rings of the tree show up as lines on this core sample. Scientists count these lines to determine the tree's age (see diagram).

Here's how cross dating works:

Scientists first take a core sample from a living tree that produces distinct, reliable annual rings. (Conifers growing in the American Southwest produce some of the most reliable, drought-sensitive rings. These were the trees used by scientists as they were first developing cross-dating techniques.) By counting backward starting with the outer ring (the current year), they can assign each ring a year, then figure out when the tree sprouted and how old it is.

The next step in cross dating is to find an older tree to compare with the younger tree. The older tree must be the same kind of tree (similar kinds of trees have similar kinds of growth rings), must grow or have grown in the same area, and must have been alive for part of the time that the younger tree was growing up. (In cross dating, scientists often use stumps, logs, beams in old buildings, or any part of a tree trunk that clearly shows the annual rings.)

Dendrochronologists then compare the inner (oldest) rings of the core sample with the outer (youngest) rings of the stump or log to find a section where the ring patterns match (see diagram). Since the scientists have already assigned dates to the younger tree, they can now assign the same dates to the overlapping rings on the older tree. Then they can count backward to date all the rings on the older tree. By finding still older trees, and overlapping them with increasingly older trees, scientists have discovered cycles of drought from over 10,000 years ago, the dates ancient cities were built, and even the age of the wood used to frame paintings done by Rembrandt! (Cross dating is considered more accurate than radioactive carbon dating, one of the methods used to tell the age of fossils.)

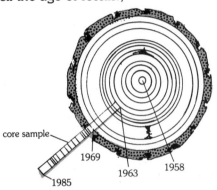

core sample
1969
1985
1963
1958

Note: In the following part of the activity, we have adapted cross-dating techniques. Dendrochronologists look at the *pattern* of rings to cross-date trees. To make it easier for the kids, we've instructed them to lay the core samples on top of the cross section to match the overlapping sections. With real trees the distances between the rings would never match perfectly. Dendrochronologists also core many trees in one area to get an accurate representative sample of the growth rings in similar trees.

Now pass out a copy of page 24 to each person. Explain that the large cross section at the top of the page is from a tree that was used to build an Oklahoma farmhouse. They must find out when the farmhouse was built by finding out when the tree started growing and when it was cut down. (The kids can assume that the farmhouse was built the same year the tree was cut.) They can also discover when some events happened during the life of the tree. To find out, they must study the core samples at the bottom of the page.

First explain what a core sample is and how a core sample is taken. Have the kids cut out each core sample, making sure they leave the lettered tabs attached. Then describe how dendrochronologists cross-date trees by matching similar ring patterns from a core sample to a cross section. Explain that only one of the three cores is from a tree that grows in the same area where the log (the cross section) once grew. It has an interval of rings that overlaps with a section of the tree trunk at the top of the page. The kids must first decide which core matches the trunk cross section.

To do this, they should take one of the core samples and try to match its pattern of lines with a section of the rings on the round cross section. (See the illustration on the left for how to do this. Remind the kids that core samples go no farther than the center of the tree, so they should not extend the core sample across the center of the cross section.)

When they've discovered which core sample overlaps the cross section (core sample B), they should count backward on the core sample to find out the actual dates when the core sample matches the cross section. Tell them that the line closest to the letter on their tab is the annual ring from 1985.

Once they determine the dates they can figure out when the tree was cut down and when it first started growing. (It was cut down in 1930 and started growing in 1896.) Tell them that county records kept during that time indicate that the farm was abandoned in 1933, only three years after it was built. What was happening in Oklahoma during this time that might have caused farmers to abandon their farms? (The Dust Bowl of the early 1930s forced many farmers to give up their farms and move to new land.)

Then have the kids assign dates to some of the events in the tree's life. What year did fire scar the tree? (1915) How many years did it take for the tree to grow around the remains of a dead branch? (10 years) How long did the drought that began in 1912 last? (two years)

Wrap up the activity by asking the kids for ideas on other things that cross dating can reveal.

COPYCAT PAGE

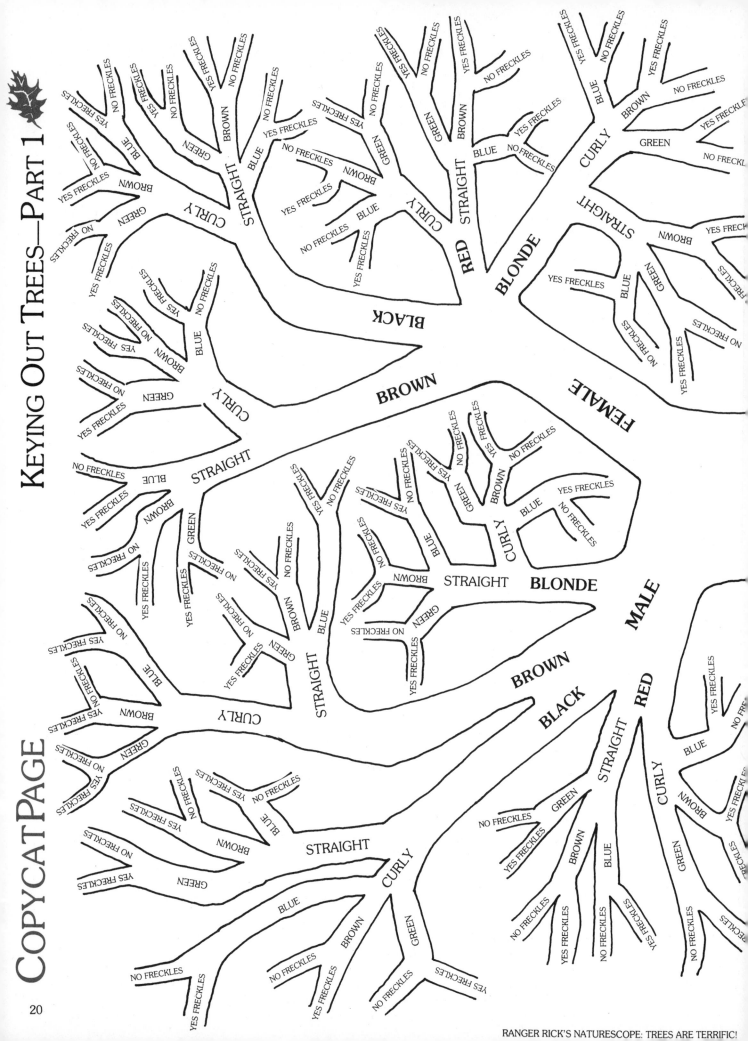

LEAF KEY

1. Leaves are shaped like needles . . . . go to **2**
Leaves are broad and flat. . . . . go to **3**

2. Long needles grow in bunches of five. . . . . WHITE PINE
Needles are short, and grow singly along the branch . . . . SITKA SPRUCE

3. Leaves are opposite . . . . go to **4**
Leaves are alternate . . . . go to **5**

4. Leaves are simple . . . . SILVER MAPLE
Leaves are compound. Leaflets grow around the stem in a circle. . . . .
HORSE CHESTNUT

5. Leaves are simple . . . . go to **6**
Leaves are compound . . . . go to **8**

6. Leaves are lobed. . . . . WHITE OAK
Leaves are toothed . . . . go to **7**

7. Leaves are long and slender . . . . WEEPING WILLOW
Leaves are rounded . . . . CHOKE CHERRY

8. Branches have thorns . . . . HONEY LOCUST
Leaflets are toothed. . . . . BLACK WALNUT

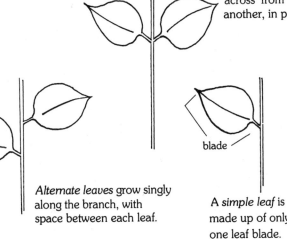

Opposite *leaves* grow directly across from one another, in pairs.

blade

leaflets

lobed

Alternate leaves grow singly along the branch, with space between each leaf.

A *simple leaf* is made up of only one leaf blade.

A *compound leaf* has many *leaflets*.

toothed

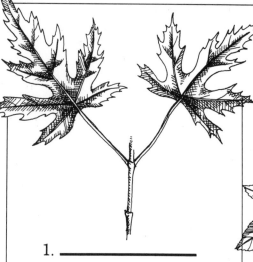

1. _____

2. _____

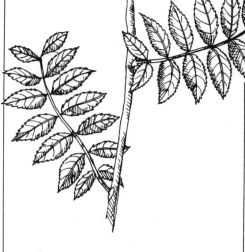

3. _____

4. _____

5. _____

6. _____

7. _____

8. _____

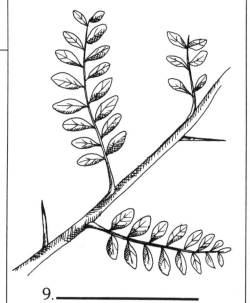

9. _____

A.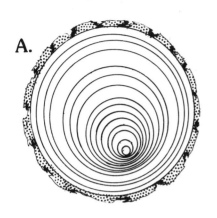

B.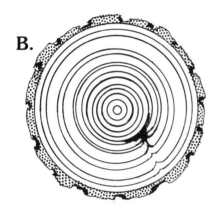

C.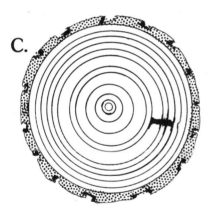

D.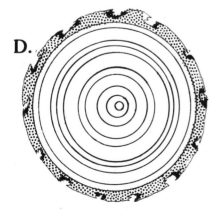

1. Fallen tree _____

2. Fire _____

3. Drought _____

4. Insect attack _____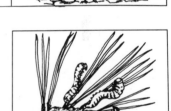

5. Construction _____

6. Growing on slope _____

7. Dead branch _____

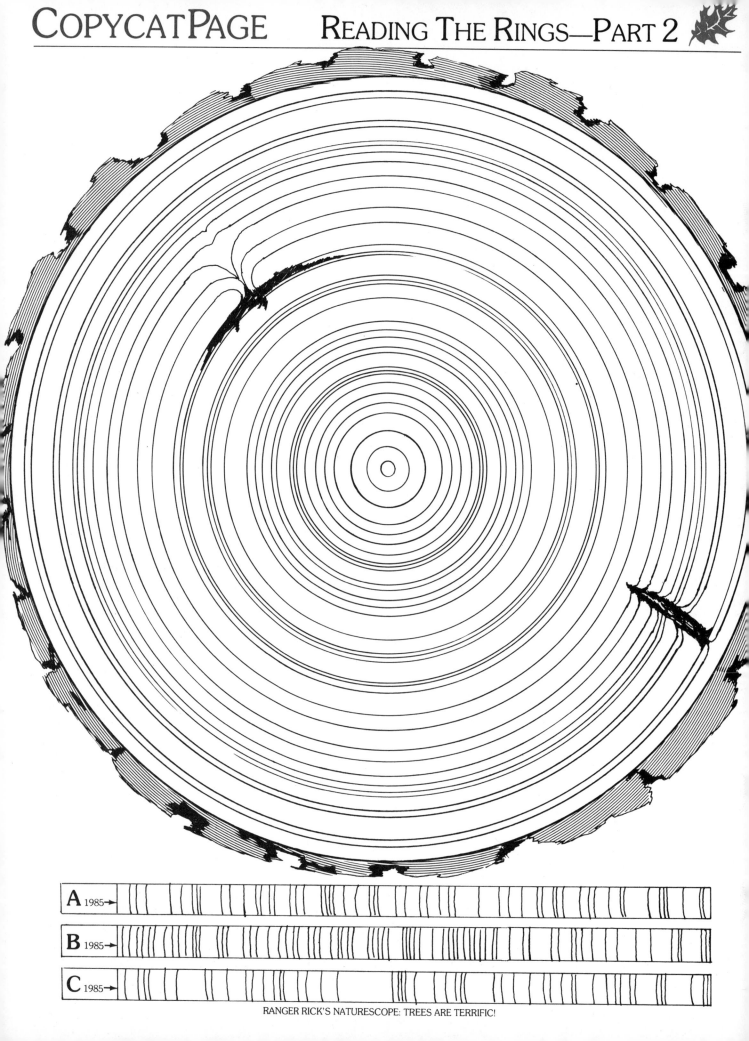

A 1985→

B 1985→

C 1985→

GROWING UP A TREE

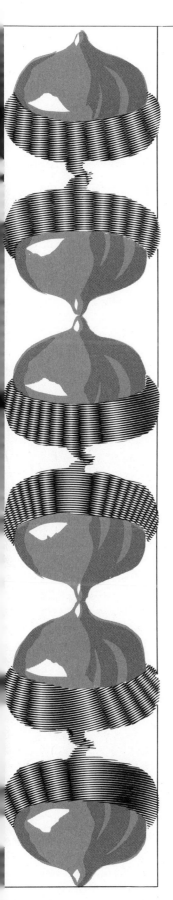

 t's late spring and the trees are loaded with pollen. Like a thick dusting of talcum powder, it covers the male cones of gymnosperms and the male flower parts of angiosperms. The pollen is ready to be swept up by the wind or carried along by bees, bats, birds, and other forest creatures.

Pollen grains are microscopic bits of life—male cells that must reach their female counterparts to do the job they were "made" for. In the case of cone-bearing trees, such as pines and firs, the pollen must land on a female cone and slide down a scale to the immature seeds (ovules) inside. With flowering trees, such as beeches, maples, and magnolias, the pollen must land on the tip of a *pistil* (female flower part containing the ovules) inside one of the flowers. For both types of trees the mission is the same—to fertilize an egg and form a mature tree seed.

FROM SEED TO SEEDLING

Starting Out a Seed: Most trees begin as seeds. And every tree, sooner or later, begins the business of producing seeds of its own.

A seed is really a tiny blueprint of the tree to come. The tiny embryo inside is complete with parts that will eventually develop into a shoot, roots, and leaves. Also included is a storehouse of energy—a supply of food in the form of starch, sugar, and fat. This food nourishes the living embryo while the seed lies dormant. After the seed germinates, or sprouts, the food supplies the embryo with energy for growth until leaves are formed and photosynthesis can begin.

Move It or Lose It: When it comes to reproduction, trees—like all plants—are big-time gamblers. Each season's production of seeds is a game of chance in which the odds of any one becoming a mature tree are about "one in a million."

A seed that ends up at the base of the parent tree may sprout there and become a seedling. With luck the seedling will become a *sapling,* or young tree. But unless the parent tree dies, is knocked down in a storm, or is cut down, the sapling has little chance of becoming a mature tree. There's usually no way it can successfully compete with the parent for enough light.

Their chances of surviving are improved if seeds can be spread to other areas, or *dispersed.* So the seeds of most trees are made to travel.

"Oh, Give Me a Home . . .": Travel, of course, has its own hazards. Seeds have many amazing ways of getting around, but they cannot control exactly *where* they go. A floating coconut, which needs to land on a sandy shore to sprout, may drift for years at sea. A maple seed sailing on the wind can end up in someone's backyard and, although it succeeds in sprouting, may fall prey to a lawn mower. A cedar seed that needs lots of sunlight may land in the shade of a deep forest. And a cottonwood tuft that needs a moist stream bank may end up on a dry, dusty roadside.

To sprout and begin growing, a seed must—by luck—fall in a place with the right amount of light, right temperature range, right amount of moisture, and sufficient and suitable soil.

Ready, Set, Grow!: If a healthy seed lands in just the right spot, it begins to grow. (Some species need to lie dormant through freezing temperatures before they can sprout; others can sprout right away.) First the seed begins to absorb water from the soil, causing the embryo inside to grow larger. Next a tiny root tip pokes its way through the seed's hard outer covering (called the *seed coat*) and digs into the soil.

(continued next page)

Soon, tiny root hairs begin to sprout along the root. These tiny strands push between particles of soil, absorbing water and minerals. The mineral-rich root sap flows up to the rest of the tiny seedling.

With a steady supply of water and minerals, the seedling next sends out a shoot. Cells inside the shoot begin to grow and multiply, sending the future tree trunk up through the soil. (Special chemicals in the shoot, called growth hormones, cause the shoot to grow *up*, against gravity.) Soon—usually within a few days—the new shoot breaks through the surface of the soil.

FROM SEEDLING TO ADULT

Laying On the Layers: Once a seedling breaks ground, it's on its way to becoming a young tree. Leaves grow and immediately begin the job of making food. During its first growing season, the young tree's phloem and xylem cells transport food, water, and minerals to all parts of the tiny seedling (see page 6 for more about the cambium, phloem, and xylem). As more woody xylem cells form, the stem becomes thicker and stronger.

It's Up to You, Bud: As a tree grows, it not only develops a thicker trunk—it also grows taller. Trees grow taller only at the tip of the trunk and at the tips of the branches. They do this by forming *terminal buds.* Each bud contains a tiny shoot that, on most trees, is wrapped in protective *bud scales.* The scales form a tough, weatherproof "suit of armor." When the bud sprouts, a new green shoot starts to grow and eventually becomes a new branch. (In climates with a cool or cold season, terminal buds form during the growing season and then lie dormant until spring.) Besides having buds on the tips of their branches, most trees also have buds that form on the *sides* of their branches.

Shutting Down for Winter: Tree growth slows as cold weather approaches, and the buds that formed during the growing season eventually become dormant. In deciduous trees, chlorophyll in the leaves gradually breaks down and photosynthesis eventually stops. Because water is not as available to trees during cold weather as it is during the growing season (it freezes and is not as easily absorbed by the roots), shutting down photosynthesis is one way deciduous trees can survive the winter. (Plants need water in order for photosynthesis to take place.) And since deciduous trees don't photosynthesize during winter, they no longer need their leaves. So deciduous trees simply get rid of their leaves as the weather turns colder. (In many tropical areas and other areas that have a wet and a dry season instead of spring, summer, winter, and fall, deciduous trees drop their leaves as the dry season approaches.)

Many evergreens survive winter or the dry season with their leaves still hanging on because they have special adaptations to compensate for scarce water supplies. For example, many evergreen leaves are covered with a thick, waxy coating that helps hold water in and prevents evaporation. Also, the leaves of some evergreens contain a kind of natural antifreeze that helps prevent injury to water-filled cells.

Making More Trees: Most trees reproduce sexually. That means male cells (formed in the pollen) unite with eggs (formed in the cones or blossoms, depending on the type of tree) to make seeds. But many trees can also reproduce *vegetatively,* which means they can grow from a part of the living tree. Some trees grow from *suckers,* which are shoots that sprout from the roots. Other trees can grow when twigs fall to the ground and eventually form roots. Many trees can also sprout from stumps.

GROWING UP A FOREST

Trees grow together in communities called *forests*. The types of trees that grow in a particular forest community depend on the climate in the area and the type of soil that is found there. Although there are thousands of species of trees in the world, scientists have divided the world's forests into four major groups:

Boreal Forests: These form a broad band across northern Canada, Europe, and Asia. Boreal forests are made up mostly of firs, spruces, and other needle-leaved trees that are adapted to cold winters and a short growing season. (These types of forests are also found in many mountainous areas where the climate is similar to that of the far north.)

Mixed Forests: South of the boreal forests are areas of mixed forests, made up of conifers and deciduous trees. Mixed forests grow across much of North America, Europe, and Asia, in areas where the climate is milder than it is in boreal areas.

Deciduous Forests: In many temperate areas broad-leaved deciduous trees such as beech, maple, oak, and hickory form large tracts of deciduous forests. (Deciduous forests often contain some pines, hollies, and other evergreens, but these usually aren't the dominant trees.) In the past, much of North America and parts of Europe were covered with unbroken tracts of deciduous forests.

Tropical Forests: These forests, which grow in parts of Central and South America, Africa, Asia, and Australia, form a broad band around the equator. Because they grow in areas where there are warm temperatures year round, long hours of daylight, and lots of rain, these forests are lush and productive. Most of the trees that grow in these forests are broad-leaved evergreens. (See pages 50 and 52 for more about tropical forests.)

Bruce Norfleet

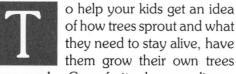

Grow a Sprout!

Plant tree seeds and observe how they grow.

Objectives:
Describe a tree seedling's roots and stem. Discuss the things tree seeds and seedlings need in order to grow.

Ages:
Primary

Materials:
- *several citrus fruits*
- *styrofoam cups (one for each person)*
- *sand or half-and-half mixture of soil and perlite*
- *several small spoons*
- *ballpoint pen*
- *toothpicks (optional)*
- *avocado seeds (optional)*
- *glass jars (optional)*
- *Billy B. Sings About Trees, an album by Bill Brennan (see page 75 for details on how to order)*

Subject:
Science

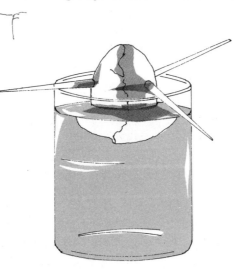

To help your kids get an idea of how trees sprout and what they need to stay alive, have them grow their own trees from seeds. Grapefruits, lemons, limes, oranges, and other citrus trees are some of the easiest trees to grow indoors—and of these, grapefruit trees are the fastest growers.

To get started, bring in (or have the kids bring in) several grapefruits or other citrus fruits. (Most grapefruits sold in grocery stores are "seedless," but these usually have at least a few seeds. Use only the largest seeds.) Set up two or three "planting stations" around the room, each with the following materials:

- styrofoam cups with several holes punched in the bottoms
- soil mixture or sand (To avoid microorganisms that could damage the seeds or young plants, get soil or sand from a store instead of digging it up.)
- small spoons for filling cups with soil mixture
- fruit seeds from a grapefruit or other citrus fruit (To avoid damaging the seeds, peel the fruit and break apart the sections instead of cutting through them with a knife. Also, put the seeds in a container of water to keep them from drying out.) If possible, use seeds that have already started to sprout inside the fruit.

Have the kids go up to the planting stations in groups of two or three. Each person can plant his or her own seed in one of the cups by filling the cup most of the way with the soil mixture or sand, laying a seed on top, and then covering it with another ½ inch (1.25 cm) of soil or sand. (Tell the kids not to pack the soil down.) Have the kids write their names on their cups with a ballpoint pen.

When everyone's finished planting, put the cups in a very warm (but not too sunny) spot. Add enough water to the soil to make it moist but not soaking wet, and make sure the soil never dries out completely. The seeds should sprout within a few weeks. (If some seeds don't sprout, have the kids replace them with fresh seeds. You can get a grapefruit seed to sprout within three to four days or so by gently peeling off the seed's covering with a razor blade before you plant it. Be sure to start peeling from the seed's rounded end and to be especially careful when you reach the seed's pointed end, where the embryo is.) As the seeds grow, discuss with the kids how seeds develop and the things seedlings need in order to grow. (See the background information on pages 25–27.)

Another good "grow-your-own" tree is the avocado. By suspending an avocado seed in water, your kids will be able to see how a seedling's stem *and* roots grow. Just peel the brown papery covering away from the seed, poke three toothpicks into it at equal distances from one another, and let the seed rest in a glass of lukewarm water with its *large end* submerged. Make sure the water doesn't evaporate to the point where it no longer covers the bottom of the seed, and replace the water with fresh lukewarm water once a week. Avocados take about three weeks to sprout. When the avocado's stem and roots are several inches long, it needs to be planted in a pot that's about one inch (2.5 cm) wider than the avocado.

To reinforce the things the kids are seeing as they watch their seedlings grow, play Bill Brennan's "Yippee, Hooray (I Am a Sprout)," a song included on his *Billy B. Sings About Trees* album.

Twig Detectives

Match twigs with the trees they come from and make bark rubbings from these trees.

Objectives:
Name the parts of a twig. Describe how studying twigs and bark can help identify a tree.

Ages:
Primary and Intermediate

Materials:
- *twigs from five local trees*
- *clippers or scissors*
- *drawing paper*
- *modeling clay*
- *construction paper*
- *field guides and reference books*
- *glue*
- *crayons and markers*
- *chalkboard or easel paper*
- *pencils*

Subject:
Science

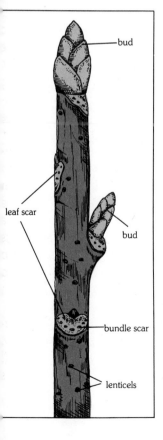

bud

leaf scar

bud

bundle scar

lenticels

How do you identify deciduous trees in winter when all the leaves have dropped off? The easiest way is to look at the twigs and bark. Even in summer and fall, while the leaves are still on the trees, the twigs and bark can be a big help in identifying a tree.

In this activity, your group will take a close-up look at the parts of a twig and then go outside to look at the twigs and bark of some common trees. Before you begin, collect a twig from five different types of trees growing in your area. (Pick common trees that you can identify.) Then cut the twigs so that they are about four inches (10 cm) long.

Divide the group into five teams and give each team a twig from a different type of tree. Then pass out a small lump of modeling clay to each group and have the kids push the bases of their twigs into the clay. Tell them to position the twigs so that everyone in the group can see them. Then copy the diagram of the twig (on the left) onto the chalkboard or a large piece of easel paper. Pass out paper and pencils and have the kids sketch and label the parts of their twigs as you talk about them.

Buds: Parts of the twig that contain the growing material for the next season. Buds grow on the tips and on the sides of twigs. Buds can contain growing material for new shoots and/or flowers.

Buds come in many shapes, textures, and colors. Most are covered with protective scales. Others are protected by overlapping leaves. In temperate areas, you can see buds throughout the year, except when young branches are emerging from the buds in the spring.

Leaf scars: Marks left by leaves that have fallen off the twig. The scars vary in position (alternate, opposite, or whorled) according to the leaf pattern of the tree. Bundle scars are the circles or lines you see on the surface of leaf scars. These marks show where the leaf's food and water "pipelines" brought water into the leaf and carried food out of the leaf. (See background on page 6 for information about xylem and phloem.)

Bark: Outer covering of twigs, branches, roots, and trunk. Bark comes in different colors and textures. Sometimes it is covered with small white dots called *lenticels*. (Lenticels allow air to flow into the cells of the tree.) The bark on a twig often looks different from the bark on the trunk. That's because the twig bark is younger and thinner. Twig bark can be used to help identify trees, but the bark on the trunk is more indicative of the type of tree. (Explain that even the bark on the trunk varies from tree to tree, because bark characteristics change as a tree matures.)

Now tell the children that they will be going outside to do two things: Find a tree that has twigs that match the ones they drew, and then make bark rubbings of the tree's bark. Before you go outside, explain how to do a bark rubbing. The kids will each hold a piece of white paper against the bark of a tree and lightly rub with a dark crayon. (You can also have the kids press pieces of clay against the bark to make a three-dimensional impression.)

Now take the teams on a group walk to find the five trees. (Have them bring their sketches along, as well as their team twig.) As you stop at each tree, tell the kids the name of that tree. As they examine the tree's twigs, they should check to see if their drawings and team twig match the twigs on the tree. If they think they have a match, have them point out the characteristics that helped them decide.

After you've looked at all five trees, pass out paper and crayons or clay. Tell the kids to return to their tree and make a rubbing or clay impression of the bark.

As a follow-up to the activity, have the kids glue their bark rubbing and twig illustration to a large piece of construction paper. Tell them to use field guides and reference books to find out what the leaves and fruit of their trees look like. Then pass out crayons and markers and have the kids draw the leaves and fruit of their tree on the construction paper. Label and hang these identification murals around the room so everyone can learn to identify these five trees all year round.

Trees Around the World

Match clues to pictures of some special trees around the world.

Objectives:
Name three unusual trees. Discuss a special feature of each of these trees. Point out on a map where these trees grow.

Ages:
Intermediate and Advanced

Materials:
- *copies of page 33 and the clues below*
- *reference books*
- *map of the world*
- *tape*
- *scissors*

Subjects:
Science and Geography

Can you imagine a tree that's as old as the pyramids? What about a tree with "knees"? In this activity your kids can learn about these and other unusual kinds of trees. They can also brush up on their geography skills by pointing out on a map where the trees grow.

Divide your group into teams of four and give each child a copy of page 33 and the clues below. Explain to the kids that they'll be using research books to match each of the pairs of clues below with the picture of the tree on page 33 that the clues describe. The first clue in each pair tells about a special characteristic of that tree, and the second clue refers to the place where the tree grows.

You can give the teams time to do a little research each day, or you can have them work completely on their own time. To match the clues with the pictures, have the kids write the number of each clue pair in the space provided under each picture. (All of the members of a team can work on all of the clues, or each child in a team can be responsible for finding the answers to two or three of the clues.) Tell the kids that they should also make sure they can find the area on a world map where each tree grows. To add an extra challenge, you might want to set a time limit.

When you're ready to go over the answers with the kids, cut out the tree pictures on page 33 and spread them out on a desk or table, along with a roll of tape. Display a map of the world in a place where everyone can see it. Then read the first set of clues and ask one of the teams if they can say which tree the clues refer to. Discuss their answers (correct answers are listed on the inside back cover), then have one or two of the members from the team find the appropriate picture from the ones you've cut out. Next have them tape the picture to the map in the correct country or state. Call on another team for the answer to the next set of clues, and continue until all the tree pictures have been placed "around the world."

AROUND THE WORLD CLUES

1.
- *one of the oldest living things in the world*
- *grows in the U.S. in a state where one of the largest and rarest birds in North America (a type of vulture) lives*

2.
- *trunk can have a circumference of 40 feet (12 m)*
- *world's largest desert is located on the continent where this tree grows*

3.
- *lives in swampy habitats and has "knees" that stick out of the water*
- *the mouth of the Mississippi River is located in one of the states where this tree grows*

4.
- *roots grow down from this tree's branches*
- *Bombay is a major city in the country where this tree grows*

5.
- *can store hundreds of gallons of water to help it survive in times of drought*
- *grows in parts of Mexico, California, and in the U.S. state that contains one of the deepest natural wonders in the world*

6.
- *twisted branches and spiny leaves might make this tree a challenge for even a monkey to climb*
- *is a native of the southernmost South American country*

7.
- *was abundant when the dinosaurs were alive*
- *is a native of the country where gunpowder, silk, and paper were first made*

8.
- *one of the tallest trees in the world*
- *wombats and koalas are native to the continent where this tree grows*

9.
- *some bulletin boards and bottle "stoppers," and also the centers of baseballs, are made from a part of this tree*
- *one of the main countries this tree grows in is the same country Christopher Columbus set sail from in 1492*

Mini-Tree Care

Learn how to care for trees by building a miniature tree from a branch.

Objectives:
Practice pruning, watering, feeding, spraying, weeding, and thinning.

Ages:
Intermediate

Materials:
One set for every 3-4 students; alternatively, one for teacher demonstration
- *fresh branches carefully pruned from trees or shrubs, with several side twigs, preferably with green leaves; one large branch (3-4 feet long), one small (2 feet). (Alternative material: corrugated cardboard, cut out in similar shapes; can be any size).*
- *flower pot (alternate: cardboard in shape of pot)*
- *modeling clay to fill pot at least halfway*
- *sod clumps or green Easter basket grass*
- *Halloween spider web or white string*
- *paper punch*
- *pruning shears*
- *pipe cleaners, 2 colors, cut in 2-inch pieces*
- *poster paints, yellow and brown*
- *spray bottle (empty)*
- *rolled oats*
- *watering can or cup (empty)*

Subject:
Science

In the activity, have the children assemble their Mini Tree using the materials listed, and explain what each item represents as you go. Press the modeling clay into the bottom of the flower pot; this represents the soil trees grow in. Press the two branches into the clay, as if they were little trees (see diagram). (Trim the "tree" bottom shorter if it is top-heavy.) Add sod clumps or Easter basket grass around the top of the pot; these represent weeds.

Now work only on the larger "tree": To make damaged branches, carefully break over one of the side twigs, and break off one altogether, leaving a stub. Add a "tent caterpillar nest" by tangling spiderweb in the tip of one other branch, and add a few pieces of one color of pipe cleaner to represent the caterpillars. Punch holes in leaves on one twig, and bend a few pieces of the second color of pipe cleaner on that twig as chewing worms. Paint a few of the leaves yellow and a few brown, to show that the tree is hungry or thirsty.

Now it's time to read the signs and give the trees what they need. First, explain that having the two trees so close together makes them crowded, and they compete for food and water so that neither can grow very well. **Thin** them by pulling out or cutting off the smaller branch.

Next, **prune** the branches as in the diagram, cutting the broken branch back to the nearest healthy twig or leaf, or if there isn't one, to the "trunk"; this helps it to heal cleanly and leave no wound. Prune the stub back to the trunk too, so it won't harbor insects, disease, or rot. And prune off the twig with the spiderweb and tent caterpillar.

Next, **"weed"** out the sod clumps or Easter grass from around the base. Weeding helps remove competition for nutrients and water.

To help the yellow-colored (painted) leaves that say the tree needs food, add **fertilizer**, in the form of rolled oats. Explain that real fertilizer would be compost or manmade fertilizer.

For the brown leaves that show the tree is thirsty, **"water"** the trees with the watering can or cup (keep it empty to avoid mess).

To control insect pests—the caterpillars near the holey leaves—**spray** a *little* "pesticide" from the water spray bottle. Explain that there is one spray called Bt, of *Bacillus thuringiensis*, that only kills the worms, and we should only use as little or any pesticide as we can. Not all bugs are bad or harm trees, and we don't want to get rid of them, too.

Now your tree, if it were a real one, would be ready to grow! What else would a real tree need to grow well (sunlight, space outside, regular water, proper planting, etc.)?

This activity can be made more advanced and realistic if done outside with a real tree, with permission of the owner.

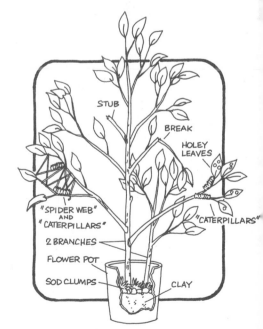

Maple Seed Mix-Up

Play a running game to learn what a tree seed needs to sprout and grow.

Objective:
Discuss the different factors that help or hinder the growth of tree seeds.

Ages:
Intermediate

Materials:
- **paper and a pencil or pen**

Subject:
Science

FAVORABLE CONDITIONS:

good soil (4)
sunlight (4)
warm spring days (4)
water (4)

HAZARDS:

drought (1)
hungry deer (1)
lawn mower (1)
poor soil (1)

Tree seeds are adapted in many ways that increase their chances of sprouting. Most, for example, have special ways of getting to a place where they might be able to grow. Yet whether a seed ends up in a place where it can sprout and grow is really a matter of chance. That's why, out of the millions of seeds a tree may produce during its lifetime, only a small percentage will ever become trees.

Your kids can get an idea of how "chancy" a tree seed's existence is, and also learn about the things seeds need to grow, by playing "Maple Seed Mix-Up." But before you begin, write the favorable conditions and hazards listed in the margin on small slips of paper. Also write the words *maple seed* on at least two slips. Then put all of the slips into a hat. (*Note:* The numbers in parentheses after each word are examples of the number of slips you can make for each hazard or favorable condition. You may need to adjust these numbers, depending on the size of your group. But don't add a lot of hazards—too many of them will make the game too hard to win.)

Next lead a discussion about the things most tree seeds need in order to sprout. (water, sunlight, good soil, and warm spring days) Explain that most seeds never sprout because they land in an area where the conditions aren't right. (See page 25 for background information.) Even if a seed does land in a place where it can sprout, the seedling may not survive for very long. A deer may eat it, joggers may crush it as they run by, and so on.

Now tell the kids that they'll be playing a running game. In the game two or more people will play the part of maple seeds. Everyone else will play the part of either a favorable condition or a hazard. (Read the list of favorable conditions and hazards to the group and discuss which are which.) Explain that the object of the game is for the "maple seeds" to "land" in a place that's free from hazards and has the conditions maple seeds need in order to sprout and grow. But, just as with real

maple seeds in nature, the places where the human maple seeds land will be a matter of chance.

When you're ready to play, take the kids to a large open area (either a big room or an area outside). Designate four bases that are located equal distances apart. (If you're playing inside, the corners of a room will work well.) Then have each child draw a slip of paper from a hat to find out what role he or she will be playing in the game. Tell the kids to keep their roles a secret, and have them hang onto the slips so you can use them again later.

Now the fun begins! Slowly count to ten and have the children run around the bases (in either direction) as you count. When you get to ten, each child should stop, then quickly go and stand near the base he or she is closest to. (Make sure they don't all bunch up around one or two of the bases.)

Once the kids have settled into place, ask the ones playing the parts of maple seeds to raise their hands. The group or groups without maple seeds can't win—they represent sites the seeds did not land on. Next have the other kids in the groups containing maple seeds reveal what parts they're playing. (It's OK if both of the seeds end up in the same group.) If a group includes one or more hazards, the group does not win. But if a group has no hazards and includes at least one of each of the favorable conditions, then the group is a winner. When a group wins, point out the fact that the person playing the part of the maple seed landed in the right spot purely by chance. The same thing happens to seeds in nature.

You may have to play the game several times before a seed ends up in just the right group. Before you play a new game, have the kids put their slips back into the hat; then have them draw new parts to play. (To make it easier for a group to win, you might want to delete one or two of the hazards and add a few more favorable conditions.)

Baobab Tree —

Saguaro Cactus —

Eucalyptus Tree —

Monkey Puzzle Tree —

Ginkgo Tree —

Bald Cypress —

Bristlecone Pine —

Cork Oak Tree —

Banyan Tree —

THE FOREST COMMUNITY

P erched on a tree limb more than 100 feet (30 m) above the forest floor, Donald Perry found himself surrounded by a world of colorful orchids, exotic "air plants," and strange animals rarely seen by human eyes. There were unusual lizards that jumped from limb to limb, brilliantly colored parrots that somehow blended right in with the treetop foliage, and slow-moving sloths whose fur had turned green with the algae that lived on it.

Perry, a tropical biologist, was researching the upper reaches of a Costa Rican rain forest. Using a unique system of ropes and pulleys, he moved among the treetops and hoisted himself up and down between high branches and the forest floor. And as he traveled in his makeshift "elevator," he saw that the plants and animals that lived in the leafy branches were very different from the ones that lived on the forest floor. In fact, he observed many "layers of life"—each with plants and animals that were specially adapted to living at certain heights in the forest.

The Costa Rican forest Perry observed is just one example of a forest community. Like all forest communities, it's made up of certain species of trees, other plants, and animals that are specially suited to living in it. And as in other forest communities, hundreds of plant and animal interactions occur there every day.

FORESTS FROM THE TOP DOWN

In one sense, a forest—whether it's a stretch of tropical rain forest in Costa Rica or a wooded hillside in Vermont—is several communities in one. That's because all forests are made up of layers of plants. Below is a look at some of the layers that might be found in a forest, starting with the forest's "roof" and working down. (The number and kinds of layers vary from forest to forest, depending on the types of trees and other plants that grow there.)

On Top of It All: Made up of the branches and leaves of the tallest trees, a forest's *canopy layer* can be 100 feet (30 m) or more above the ground. A lot of sunlight hits the canopy, making this layer a huge food-making factory where most of the forest's photosynthesis takes place.

Beneath the Big Ones: Growing under the canopy trees may be shorter trees that make up the *subcanopy layer*. Some of these trees are offspring of the canopy trees, and they may eventually become part of the canopy too. Other understory trees are smaller, altogether different species that are adapted to growing in shade.

Low-down Plants: Of course, trees aren't the only plants that grow in a forest. Beneath a forest's subcanopy, for example, may grow a *shrub layer*. Shrubs are usually smaller than trees and have many woody stems, instead of the one main stem that trees have.

At the Bottom: Ferns, grasses, wildflowers, seedling trees, and other close-to-the-ground plants are all part of a forest's *herb layer*. And hollow logs, fallen branches and leaves, lichens, and mosses are all part of the *forest floor*.

Note: Some scientists use the word *understory* to refer to the layers in a forest that grow beneath the canopy. Many biologists also include a *tree trunk layer* in the list of forest layers. That's because many birds and other creatures nest in or feed on the trunk. Also, many forest insects and other small animals spend their entire lives under the bark of a tree's trunk.

HOW MANY LAYERS?

Climate, forestry practices, soil conditions, the age of the forest, and other factors can influence the number of layers that develop in a forest. (See pages 48–50 for more about forestry.) For example, a planted stand of white pines may have only the forest floor, tree trunk, and canopy layers. A tropical rain forest, on the other hand, might have all of the layers we talked about before—plus "extras" such as an *emergent layer* of very tall trees that tower above even the canopy.

WHERE THE ANIMALS ARE

You'd never find a red squirrel building its nest on the forest floor. And even though wild turkeys can fly, you'd be unlikely to see one flying from branch to branch up in the forest canopy, searching for food. That's because most forest species usually nest, feed, and carry out their other activities in one or two of a forest's layers. For example, red squirrels are basically canopy animals, and wild turkeys spend most of their time on the forest floor. Each finds what it needs to survive in particular layers of the forest.

Even songbirds and other animals that can quickly and easily get from place to place tend to be "tied" to certain forest layers. For example, if you studied the warblers in a typical deciduous forest community in Maryland, you might find cerulean warblers living in the canopy, black-and-white warblers living on the tree trunks, Kentucky warblers living in the understory, and ovenbirds (also a type of warbler) spending most of their time on the forest floor. All of these tiny songbirds are closely related—but each is adapted to living in a different forest layer. In this way, none of the warblers competes with the others for the same food or nesting sites. (See the activity on page 36 for information on how some canopy animals are adapted to their habitats.)

THE FOREST MACHINE

You can think of a forest community as a kind of self-sufficient, living machine—constantly recycling energy and nutrients through its system. Here are the "parts" that keep things running:

Producers: The producers are the trees and other green plants that make the food needed to fuel the forest machine. (See page 7 for more about how plants make their food using energy from the sun.)

Consumers: The consumers are the animals in a forest community that either eat green plants directly or get the energy from green plants indirectly by eating animals that feed on green plants.

Decomposers: The decomposers are the fungi, bacteria, earthworms, and other organisms that break down dead material in the forest community. They recycle the forest machine's waste products, turning dead plants and animals into usable nutrients (nitrogen, phosphorus, and others) that can be absorbed by the roots of trees and other producers. (See page 41 for more about decomposition.)

Over and over again, energy and nutrients are recycled through the forest community, as they are in all communities—from producer to consumer to decomposer and back to producer. And the forest machine keeps on running year after year.

Treetop Traffic

***Make a gliding lizard
out of paper.***

___

Objective:
*Describe several ways
animals are adapted to
living in trees.*

Ages:
*Primary and
Intermediate*

Materials:
- *copies of pages 43
  and 44*
- *scissors*
- *tape*
- *large paper clips*
- *crayons or markers*

Subject:
Science

In this activity your group can take a close-up look at how some animals are adapted to living and moving in the trees. Then they can make their own gliding lizards to show how one tree-living animal is able to move around.

Begin by telling the children that some animals that live in the forest spend most or even all of their time in the trees. Some of these animals, such as birds, bats, and some insects, can simply fly from branch to branch or from tree to tree. But other animals have different ways of "getting around."

Next pass out a copy of page 43 to each child. Tell the kids that all of the animals on the sheet live in trees and each one has a special way of moving. Then use the information below to discuss the animals on the sheet.

CLAWS THAT HOLD ON TIGHT

- **Squirrels:** Many squirrels build their nests high up in the treetops, or *canopy*. These mammals have small claws on their feet that help them hold onto branches and tree trunks.
- **Sloths:** The sloths of Central and South American forests have long, curved claws on their feet that help them hold onto branches. Being able to hold on tight is important for sloths, since these slow-moving animals walk, sleep, mate, feed on leaves, shoots, and fruit, and even give birth while hanging upside down from branches.
- **Iguanas (ih-GWA-nas):** Some Central and South American iguanas live in the rain forest canopy, searching for flowers, leaves, insects, and other foods. These reptiles use their long, sharp claws to dig into branches as they climb.

TAILS THAT GRAB

- **Monkeys:** Some monkeys have tails that they can use as an extra hand to help them climb through the trees. This "hand" helps monkeys swing through the trees to look for fruit and leaves. The spider monkeys of Central and South America can even use their tails to pick up certain food items.
- **Tamanduas (tuh-MAN-dwas):** Tamanduas are Central and South American anteaters that have long tails and sharp claws. They use their claws to defend themselves or to rip apart ant and termite nests. And tamanduas use their long tails to hold onto branches as they move about in the treetops.

TOES THAT STICK

- **Tree Frogs:** Some Central and South American tree frogs spend their whole lives in trees. These climbing tree frogs have expanded toe tips that help them hold onto and climb trees.
- **Tarsiers (TAR-see-urs):** In the tropical rain forests of Malaysia and Indonesia, kitten-sized tarsiers leap through the trees hunting insects. They have friction pads on the ends of their toes that help them grab onto tree trunks and branches.

LEAPING AND GLIDING

- **Flying Squirrels:** Flying squirrels are found in the forests of North America, Asia, and Africa and usually feed on seeds, nuts, and insects. These squirrels have special flaps of skin that extend from their front legs to their hind legs. When they leap off a branch the flaps of skin stretch out like sails and help them glide. Flying squirrels also have claws that help them hold onto and climb trees once they land.
- **Flying Dragons:** These insect-eating lizards live in the rain forests of Asia. They have extra flaps of skin along the sides of their bodies that help them glide.
- **Flying Snakes:** These unusual Southeast Asian snakes feed on lizards. They are able to spread their ribs and flatten their bodies to become gliders.

Note: These three types of animals are not true fliers, as most birds, insects, and bats are. They are *gliders* and can't travel through the air for long periods of time.

Now pass out a copy of page 44 to each child and tell the children that they're going to make their own flying dragons. Here's how to do it:

1. Color the lizard and the tail on page 44. Then cut them out along the *thick, solid black lines.*

2. Lay the paper down with the lizard side facing you and fold along line A so that the drawing "disappears." Make a crease.

3. Unfold the glider, turn it over (lizard side down), and fold back along the B lines. (The two number 1s should meet on the backside of the glider, along the crease you made in step 2.)

4. Without unfolding step 3, fold back along line C. (The point labeled 2 should meet the two number 1 corners.)

5. Turn the glider over so that the lizard side is facing you again. Refold along line A. (You should not be able to see the lizard anymore.)

6. Lay the glider down on its side so that the "open" side faces you. (The crease should be facing away from you.)

7. Slowly lift up the top sheet and fold back along line D.

8. Fold the other side of the glider back along line D as in step 7.
9. Use a small piece of tape to attach the tail to the lizard where the Ds meet at the "tail" end. (The tail should just cover the white tip.)
10. Cut along line E—underneath the nose of the glider—and then tape the loose pieces in place.

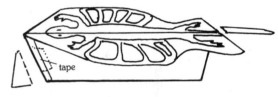

11. Attach a large paper clip to the underside of the glider at the asterisks (*). (You may need to move the paper clip up or down to improve the lizard's flight.)
12. Hold along the bottom crease where line E, the 2, and the 1s meet.

Now launch your gliding lizard and watch it sail!

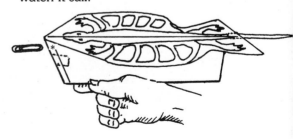

A Walk in the Woods

Listen to a rhyming story to discover how the animals in a forest use trees.

Objectives:
Explain why trees are important to wildlife. Describe two ways animals use trees.

Ages:
Primary

Materials:
- *"Read-to-me" rhyming story on page 39*
- *copies of page 45*
- *map of the United States*
- *pencils*
- *crayons or markers*
- *pictures of a hairy woodpecker, porcupine, Douglas squirrel, goshawk, and banana slug*

Subject:
Science

Here's a fun way to help the children in your group understand how trees are important to wildlife. First ask the children if they can think of any ways that trees help animals survive. (Trees are sources of food, nesting sites and materials, and shelter.) Then tell them to listen carefully as you read a rhyming story about the animals that live in a forest in Washington State. (Have someone point to Washington State on a map of the United States.) If possible, show the kids pictures of the animals they'll be hearing about in the story (see list of materials), then explain that when the story is finished they'll get a chance to vote on their favorite animal.

After reading the story pass out a copy of page 45 to each child. Tell the kids that the animals that were mentioned in the story are shown in the picture. The circles at the bottom of the page represent the different ways the animals in the story used trees. Then ask if anyone can match an animal in the picture to one of the circles below, based on what happened in the story.

As you discuss each relationship, have the kids draw a line from the animal to the picture that represents how the animal used a tree. Be sure to explain that some of the animals use trees for more than one purpose but that in the story each one was seen doing only one thing. You can use the information below to help in your discussion. Afterward, let the children color the pictures.

INFORMATION ABOUT THE ANIMALS

Porcupine: Primarily nocturnal. Climbs trees to escape predators, to rest, and to feed. May rest in hollow trees or logs. Feeds on the inner bark of trees as well as on buds, small twigs, berries, grasses, and other plant material.

Banana Slug: Feeds on all kinds of decaying vegetation and fungi. Often spends dry days on or under moist logs. May be greenish, yellow, or even white and may or may not have spots. Some can stretch their bodies out to a length of about 1 foot (30 cm)! (For pictures, see page 22 of "Snail Without a Shell," *Ranger Rick*, April 1979.)

Douglas Squirrel: Builds summer nest in trees using twigs, bark, and other materials. Nests in tree cavities in winter. Eats seeds and nuts and sometimes stores food in moist places.

Goshawk: Builds nest in trees using sticks, twigs, and bark. Feeds mainly on small mammals and birds.

Hairy Woodpecker: Eats many insects, including wood-boring insects that it catches by drilling into trees. Chisels out nest cavity in trees.

Alvin E. Staffan

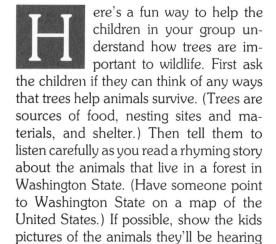

porcupine

A WALK IN A FOREST IN WASHINGTON STATE

In the forests of Washington, some people say,
Are the most wonderful creatures alive today.
Who are these creatures? And what makes them so neat?
Is it how they all look or what they all eat?
Is it how they grow up, or move all about?
Jenny and I were going to find out.

We went to the forest, a curious pair,
Intent to find out what exactly lived there
And which of the creatures, whether big, tall, or small,
Was the most fabulous, interesting creature of all.

As we walked through the forest, we heard a sharp sound—
It went "tat-a-tat-tat," and we looked all around.
Then high on a tree trunk we saw a strange bird,
And we knew right away it was he that we'd heard—
A lively woodpecker, dressed mostly in black,
With some red on his head and some white on his back.
His long, sticky tongue poked into each hole,
And caught juicy grubs that he swallowed down whole.

As we watched the woodpecker "tat-a-tat" at that tree,
We heard a soft rustling—and what did we see?
A fat little porcupine, all covered with quills.
She went shuffling by as we stood very still.
She had tiny black eyes and a short little snout,
And two big front teeth which, beyond any doubt,
She used like a chisel to tear tree bark away,
So she could eat the bark's insides, then go on her way.

Then all of a sudden, we saw a gray blur.
It was a squirrel on the run, with reddish-gray fur.
He scampered around underneath the fir trees,
Then he ran up a tree trunk, as quick as you please.
He snipped off two fir cones that fell down—*smash, crash!*
And he ran down again, just as fast as a flash.
Then he picked up a fir cone and started to feed,
And we watched as he gobbled down seed after seed.

We left the squirrel munching, and went on our way.
And then I caught sight of a sleek bird of prey.
"A goshawk!" I whispered, "On a branch in that tree."
And I pointed ahead so that Jenny could see.
"Goshawks," said Jenny, "need forests like these.
They hunt forest creatures and nest in the trees."
The goshawk just sat there and gave us a stare,
Before flying off, to go hunting somewhere.

On a log in the distance Jenny spied something weird,
And we ran to get closer before it disappeared.
You'll never guess what we saw in that log when we came:
A big yellow slug—called a banana slug by name.
It was six inches long and all covered with goo,
And its skin was bright yellow with small black spots too.
The slug nibbled a mushroom, then crawled slowly away
Leaving slime as it slid, every inch of the way.

The slug wasn't alone on that log on the ground.
There were dozens of creatures all crawling around.
When we peeled off some bark to see what lived inside,
We saw pill bugs and beetles and a mouse that had died.
There were millipedes and centipedes, a long-legged spider,
And a shiny black cricket that was longer than wider.
There was so much more life than we thought there would be,
Living under the bark of that old dead tree!

It was getting quite late and we just couldn't stay.
We'd seen so many creatures—it had been a great day!
But which was the neatest? *We* hadn't a clue.
We tried to decide, but . . . well, what would you do?

Under Cover!

Take a look at the animals that use a tree by making a "peek-a-tree."

Objective:
Describe three ways trees are important to wildlife.

Ages:
Primary and Intermediate

Materials:
- *copies of pages 46 and 47*
- *small, pointed scissors*
- *crayons or markers*
- *blank sheets of paper*
- *pencils (optional)*
- *tape*
- *stapler*

Subject:
Science

 ere's a fun way for kids to discover some of the many ways animals use trees. First pass out a copy of page 47 to each child and explain that all of the animals in the picture use trees or the areas around them for shelter, for food, or as a nesting site. Then tell them that they probably wouldn't find all of these animals on the same tree at the same time. That's because animals use trees for different things during different times of the year and they tend to spread themselves out among different trees so they'll have plenty of room.

As you discuss the animals in the picture you can use the information provided below. Afterward, pass out copies of page 46 and let each child make his or her own "peek-a-tree." *Note:* In the discussion below, the names of the animals that appear on pages 46 and 47 are in italics.

HIDDEN BY THE LEAVES

A Place to Rest: Many birds use trees as resting spots. For example, the *barred owl* may rest in the branches of a tree during the day or may perch there at night to look and listen for mice and other prey.

Nesting High: A fork in a tree may be a perfect place for a *rose-breasted grosbeak* to build its nest. Many other birds and some other animals such as squirrels also build their nests in the branches of trees.

A Treetop Smorgasbord: The *gray squirrel* spends most of its time in the treetops and feeds on many different nuts, seeds, and fruits. A lot of other animals also feed in the treetops.

Blending In: Some animals are well camouflaged for their life in the trees. The *walkingstick* feeds on tree leaves during the day. Looking a lot like a small stick helps this insect hide from birds and other predators. Some other tree-dwelling insects resemble leaves, thorns, or bark.

BENEATH THE BARK

Growing Up Inside a Tree: Some animals spend most of their lives beneath the bark of trees. *Bark beetles* lay their eggs in wood underneath the bark. After the eggs hatch, the larvae form patterns in the wood as they eat their way through it.

Nesting Within: Many animals nest inside trees. Birds such as the *hairy woodpecker* chisel out their own nesting holes in trees. These cavities may be used by many other forest creatures after the woodpeckers have abandoned them. *Honey bees,* flying squirrels, and some birds may build their homes (hives or nests) in abandoned woodpecker nests or in other tree cavities.

Fruiting Fungi: Many types of fungi grow on trees. The threadlike *mycelium* of these fungi often grows beneath the bark, hidden from view. But when a fungus such as the *shelf fungus* produces its fruiting body, it's easy to spot.

AROUND THE ROOTS

Feeding on the Roots: Many insects, mites, *millipedes,* and pill bugs spend part of their lives in the ground. The *cicada,* for example, spends its underground life as a nymph around the base of a tree, feeding on sap from the tree's roots. Some fungi form a "partnership" with the roots of trees. These fungi grow around the growing tips of the roots and feed on the tree's sap. The fungi aid the tree by absorbing nutrients from the soil and passing them into the tree.

Burrowing, Furrowing: *Earthworms,* moles, and many other creatures tunnel through the soil beneath a tree. As they churn up the soil they make it easier for a tree's roots to grow and absorb oxygen. Some animals such as *short-tailed shrews* and *chipmunks* dig tunnels beneath trees. And animals such as chipmunks and squirrels may store a cache of nuts in the ground near the base of a tree.

HOW TO MAKE A "PEEK-A-TREE"

1. Color sheets A and B.
2. Using pointed scissors, cut the rectangles on sheet A *on the dotted lines only.* Then fold the cut pieces back along the solid lines. (The rectangles should work like little doors.) If you're having trouble getting started, push the point of a sharp pencil through one of the corners of each rectangle. Then stick the point of the scissors through the hole and begin cutting.
3. Make a tab for each door by cutting out a small piece of paper 1 inch (2.5 cm) long by ½ inch (1.25 cm) wide. Tape half of the piece of paper

to the *back* of the door so that ½ inch (1.25 cm) hangs free and forms a tab. (Be sure to tape the piece of paper to the back of the door edge *opposite* the uncut side.) You can use the tabs to keep the doors closed by tucking them under the cut edges.

4. Put sheet A on top of sheet B and staple them together at the top and the bottom.
5. Then open the doors to see what is underneath the leaves and bark and around the roots!
6. Under the door with the chipmunk on it, draw a picture of a creature that might live in or on a rotting log.

A Rottin' Place to Live

Examine a decomposing log and then make a log mural.

Objectives:
Define decomposition.
Explain how dead trees are important to wildlife.

Ages:
Primary, Intermediate, and Advanced

Materials:
- **paper sacks**
- **leaves, twigs, and bark**
- **newspaper**
- **pencils and paper**
- **clipboards or pieces of sturdy cardboard and rubber bands**
- **magnifying glasses (one per person)**
- **jars with lids or "bug" boxes**
- **field guides**
- **easel paper**
- **yarn**
- **construction paper**
- **scissors**
- **glue or tape**
- **markers or crayons**

Subject:
Science

Have your kids take a close-up look at a dead log to learn about decomposition. Before you begin, collect some leaves, twigs, bark, and any other tree materials you can find. Put all of one kind of material into the same paper sack. (For example, put all of the leaves in one paper sack, all of the twigs in another, and so on.) Then spread out some newspaper in an area where all of the kids can gather around it.

Explain that as a tree grows it collects minerals and other nutrients from the soil and air around it. These nutrients—carbon, nitrogen, phosphorus, and some others—are used by the tree to make new bark, roots, leaves, twigs, and wood. When the tree dies the nutrients become available for animals and other plants to use. And as the nutrients are used, the tree is slowly broken down into *humus,* a dark rich layer of soil. The process of breaking down a tree into its nutrients is called *decomposition.*

Now ask the kids what parts of a tree might become part of the soil. (all parts) As they give their answers, sprinkle your samples onto the newspaper. (For example, if someone says "leaves" you can pour the leaves out of the paper sack and onto the newspaper.) When you have piled up all of your samples, ask the kids if they think the mess on the newspaper is soil. When they say "no" ask them if they know what is needed to turn it into soil. Then use the following information to explain how decomposition works.

(continued next page)

Bruce Norfleet

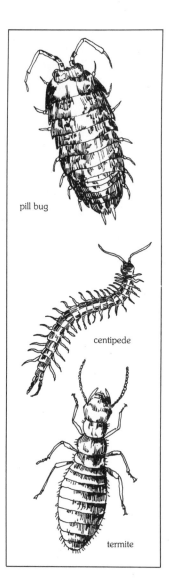

pill bug

centipede

termite

FROM DEAD TREE TO SOIL

Many things depend on dead trees for food, shelter, and/or nesting sites. Fungi, bacteria, and wood-eating insects such as termites and some beetles are usually the first to "move into" a dead tree. As they feed on the tree they help soften the wood, and the tunnels of the wood-eating insects provide access routes through which water and other fungi, bacteria, and small animals can enter the tree. Some of the animals lay their eggs in the soft wood and the larvae feed on the wood when they hatch. Others feed on the fungi or animals already living in the dead tree. And some animals make their nests or seek shelter inside decaying trees. As all of these animals excavate, eat, and burrow through trees, they help to break them down. It takes a long time to turn a tree into humus.

Now tell the kids that they are going to see decomposition in action by examining a rotting log. Before you take the group out, scout around and find an area that has several logs (or large fallen limbs) close together. Then divide the kids into groups of three or four. Give each group some magnifying glasses (one per person, if possible), four or five "bug" boxes or jars with lids, a pencil, markers or crayons, one or two sheets of paper, a clipboard,

and some field guides (to insects, spiders, reptiles, and amphibians). (If you don't have clipboards, have the kids use tape, glue, or rubber bands to attach the sheets of paper to pieces of sturdy cardboard.)

Explain to the kids that as they examine the log they should try to find at least one creature from each of these regions: on top of the log, under the bark, and underneath the log or on the ground nearby. They should use the blank sheets of paper to draw the plants, animals, and fungi that they find and write down where on the log they found each one. (Have the kids put the animals they find into jars with lids so they can observe and draw them.)

Then take the kids outside and let each group choose a log to study. (Or let several groups work together on one log.) Explain that they'll be using their drawings later to make a mural. *Note:* Before taking the kids out, be sure to set your own safety guidelines, such as: "Do not stick bare hands into dark holes, release all of the animals after observing and sketching them, and replace the log in its original position after examining it."

Afterward, go back inside and have each group explain what they found. Then set up a log mural. Here's how:

MAKING A LOG MURAL

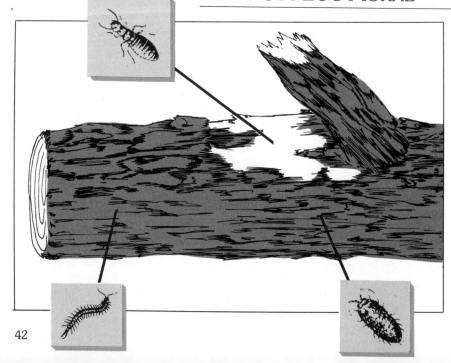

1. Tape several large pieces of easel paper together, draw a log on the paper, and then hang the picture on a bulletin board or wall.
2. Cut out the drawings the kids made outside, and glue them onto separate pieces of construction paper.
3. Tape the drawings around the log and then use pieces of yarn to connect each picture to the area on the log where the animals were found (see diagram).

COPYCAT PAGE

TREETOP TRAFFIC

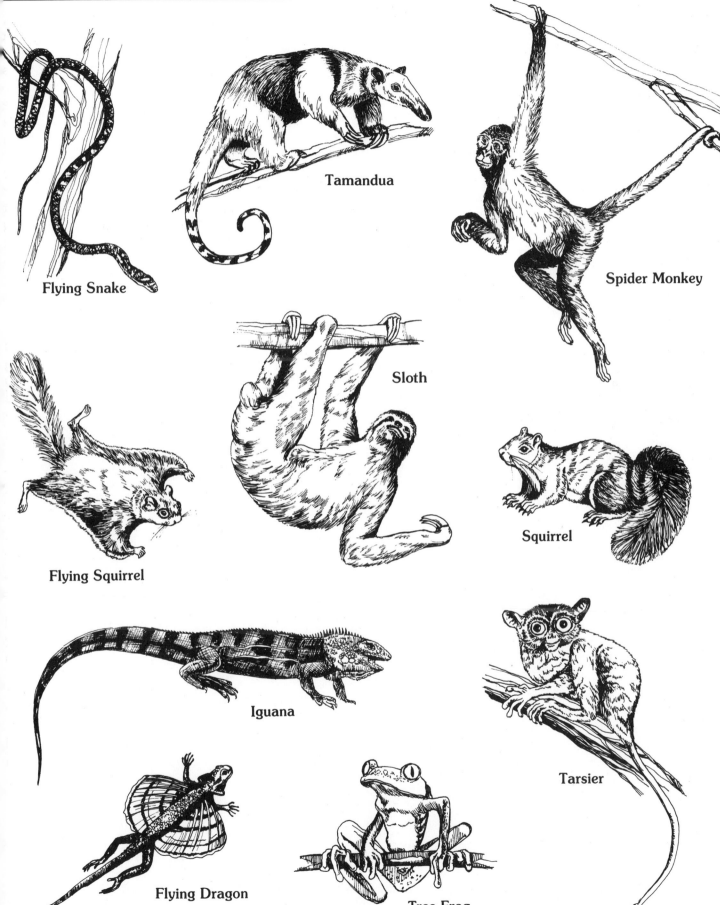

Flying Snake

Tamandua

Spider Monkey

Flying Squirrel

Sloth

Squirrel

Iguana

Tarsier

Flying Dragon

Tree Frog

Cut out along thick solid lines.

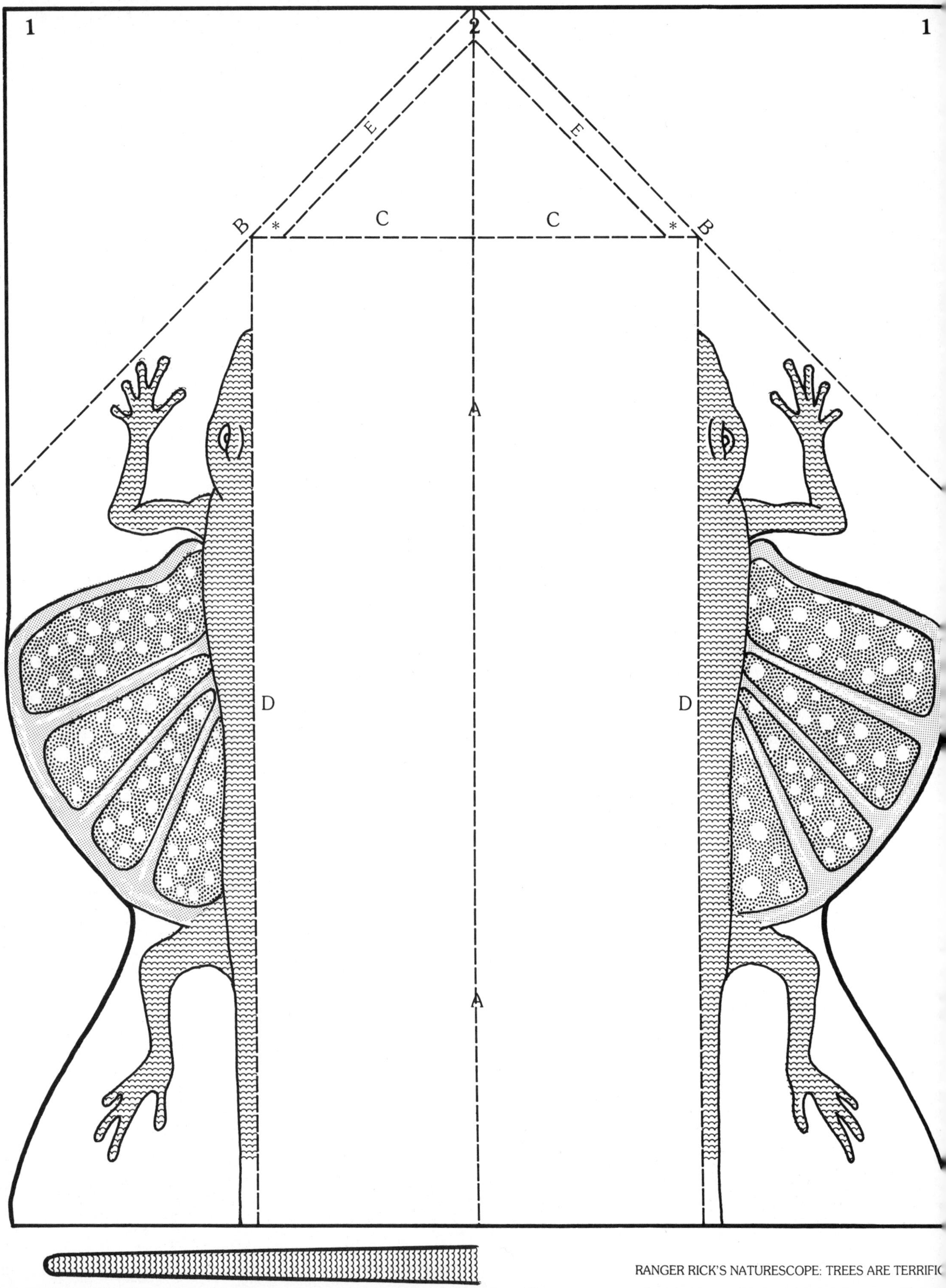

2

E   E

B   *   C   C   *   B

A

D   D

A

A Walk In The Woods

Copycat Page

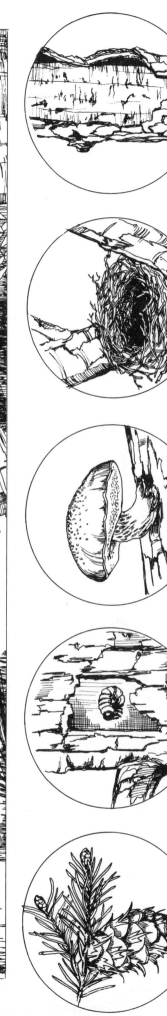

BARK

NEST

MUSHROOM

BEETLE GRUB

FIR CONE

ROSE-BREASTED GROSBEAK

HONEY BEE

HAIRY WOODPECKER

CHIPMUNK

SHELF FUNGUS

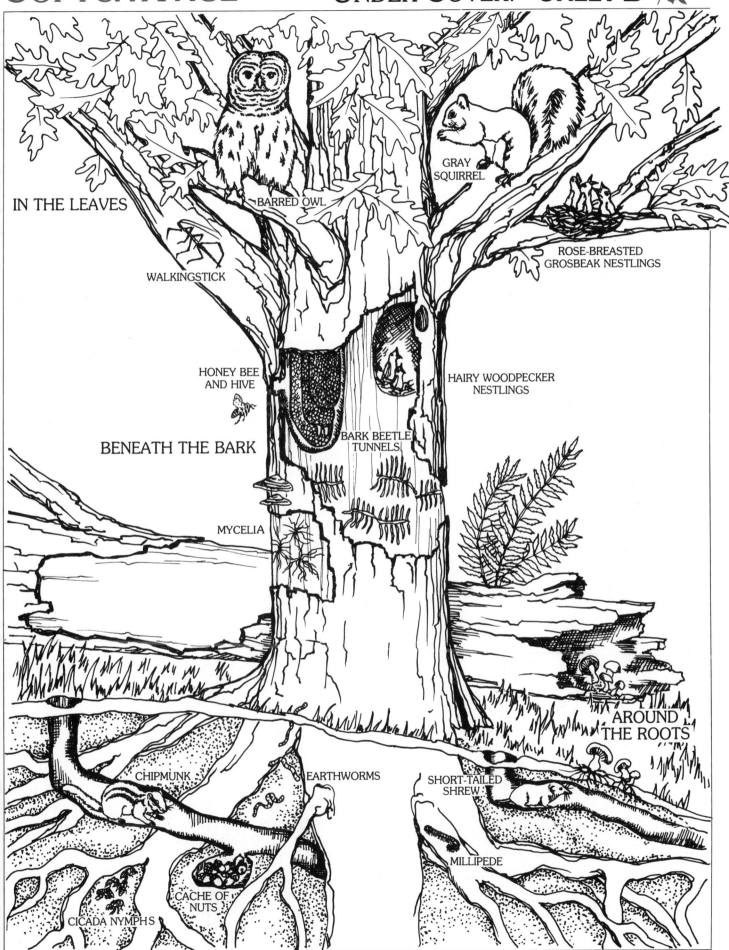

IN THE LEAVES

BARRED OWL

GRAY SQUIRREL

ROSE-BREASTED GROSBEAK NESTLINGS

WALKINGSTICK

HONEY BEE AND HIVE

HAIRY WOODPECKER NESTLINGS

BENEATH THE BARK

BARK BEETLE TUNNELS

MYCELIA

AROUND THE ROOTS

CHIPMUNK

EARTHWORMS

SHORT-TAILED SHREW

CACHE OF NUTS

MILLIPEDE

CICADA NYMPHS

RANGER RICK'S NATURESCOPE: TREES ARE TERRIFIC!

PEOPLE AND FORESTS

I t would be hard to find a natural resource that's more useful than trees. We build with trees, make all kinds of products out of them, eat their fruit, and even extract energy from them. Trees provide more than just things for people to use, though. For example, trees keep soil from eroding and provide food and homes for wildlife. And forests provide recreation for people who enjoy camping, hiking, hunting, bird watching, and so on. Because they're so important in so many ways, trees and their habitats must be carefully managed. And that's where *forestry*—the science of managing forests—comes in.

FORESTS ON THE JOB

The idea of managing trees and forests didn't occur to early American settlers and pioneers. To them, the forests of the New World took up space that could be put to "better" use if it was farmed. So many forests were often cut down, burned over, and turned into pastures and cropland. By the mid-1800s, much of America's original forestland was gone.

But finally, in the early 1900s, the science of forestry began to catch on in the United States. (Several decades earlier, France, Germany, and other European countries had started to develop forest management techniques.) And today, managers put forestry practices to work on millions of acres of forestland.

A Forestful of Paper: Not all forests are managed in the same way, though. For example, a paper company may decide that it wants to grow as many *pulpwood trees* (trees that will one day be made into paper) as it can on a tract of land that it owns. So the company would manage exclusively for pulpwood. That may mean clearing the vegetation in the area, planting a particular species of fir, pine, or other fast-growing "paper tree," protecting the seedlings from insects and diseases, and thinning the growing stand to keep invading plants from competing with the paper trees for water and nutrients. Finally, after about 25 years, the pulpwood would be cut, or *harvested,* and made into paper. (See page 65 for a rundown on how paper is made.)

Putting Wildlife into the Picture: Another paper company, on the other hand, may decide that it wants to manage a tract of land not only for pulpwood but also for wildlife. Managing for wildlife might involve allowing the natural forest to stand in certain areas, putting up nesting boxes for birds and squirrels, and planting certain wildlife food plants.

Meeting the Needs of Many: In some forests, a lot of different factors are worked into the management plan. For example, one area in a forest may be managed for pulpwood and another may be managed for trees that could eventually be cut into boards and other building materials. The forest as a whole may be managed so that certain kinds of wildlife can live in it, and also so that people can camp in it, fish in its streams, and so on. This concept of managing a forest for several different uses at one time, called *multiple use management,* is practiced mainly in state and national forests (and to a lesser extent on commercially owned and privately owned forests). These forests belong to the public, and they have to be managed to satisfy the different needs of all the people who use them.

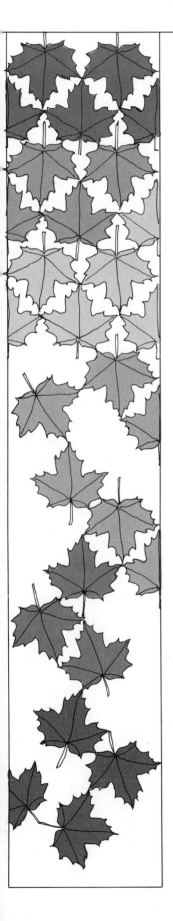

FINDING A BALANCE

It's not always easy for forest managers to satisfy all the different demands people put on forests. Sometimes two or more forest uses will clash, and the conflicts that result can be difficult to resolve. Often these conflicts center on our ever-growing use of wood products and our desire, at the same time, to preserve forests for wildlife, recreation, and other things we value. Politics often play an important role too—especially in the management of public lands. Here is one example of the kinds of controversies forest managers face:

To Cut or Not to Cut: Forests in the United States rarely reach a "ripe old age" before they're harvested. That's because it's usually more profitable to harvest a forest after, say, 40 or 50 years than it is to wait 150 years or more for the trees in the forest to grow as large as they can. But here and there in the United States are parcels of *old-growth forest*—forests made up of very old, large trees. Some of these forests have never been logged; others may have been logged so long ago that the new trees that sprouted after the old ones were cut down have since grown old themselves. The reasons these forests were allowed to become old-growth stands vary. For example, in some forests the grade of the land makes it too steep for loggers and harvesting equipment to get to. Also, a few forests are so remote that hauling wood out of them would be more expensive than it's worth.

Today new innovations in equipment are making harvesting easier, and the increased demand for wood products is fueling the drive to open up old-growth forests. (Old-growth stands in national parks and in designated wilderness areas can't legally be harvested, although the parts of these stands that stretch outside park or wilderness boundaries are "fair game.") But many people think that only very limited logging—or no logging at all—should be allowed in old-growth forests. They are concerned that rare species of wildlife dependent on these forests could eventually become extinct as their old-growth habitats are harvested. Many scientists also feel that old-growth forests should be preserved because they can often support more species of wildlife than younger forests can. And some people feel that old-growth forests should be left intact as living monuments, since they're the last remnants of the huge, "untouched" forests that once stretched over much of the country.

WARDING OFF THE THREATS

Fire, diseases, and certain types of insects can really take a toll on forests, destroying millions of acres of forestland every year. That's why protecting forests from these threats is one of the most important aspects of a forest manager's job. Here's a rundown on each of these problems:

Burn, Baby, Burn: Forest fires account for tremendous losses in timber and other forest benefits. People are responsible for most of the fires (most are accidental, but some are deliberately set), and lightning starts the rest.

Forest fires aren't always bad, though. In fact, most forest managers now recognize that fire is a natural part of many forest communities. Lightning-caused fires and other naturally occurring fires burn through some forests once every 25 years or so, and many trees in these forests benefit from the flames. In some pine forests, for example, a fire might destroy young hardwood trees that are becoming established in the forest's understory—but the pine trees might not be damaged much at all. (Many mature pine trees and some other trees have tough, fire-resistant bark.) Since pines are unable to compete with most hardwoods for sunlight, fire serves to maintain the pine forest by preventing hardwoods from "taking over" and becoming the dominant trees.

Some pines are adapted to fire by having cones that don't release their seeds until a fire passes through the forest. These cones have a gluelike resin that keeps them tightly shut. The heat of a fire melts the resin, allowing the cones to open up and drop their seeds. The ash left on the forest floor after a fire passes makes a nutrient-rich seedbed.

Blights and "Bugs": Since they're not as directly dangerous to humans as forest fires can be, diseases and insects that attack trees usually don't get as much publicity as fires do. Yet each year certain fungi, viruses, beetles, moths, and other threats together account for several times more forest damage than fire does.

Forest managers can fight these problems in several different ways. Often they use pesticides, fungicides, and other chemicals, but these can be damaging to wildlife and the ecology of the forest. So some forest managers try to keep diseases and insects in check with *biological controls*. For example, forest managers in an insect-infested area may try releasing sterile male insects. These males may breed with female insects, but any eggs the females lay will never hatch.

FORESTS FOR THE FUTURE?

Forestry is an intensive business in most of the industrialized countries of the world. That's because these countries can't afford *not* to manage a resource that provides so many benefits. Without management, forests and all the things we get from them would eventually be used up.

But in most developing countries forests aren't yet managed much at all. In fact, in many areas forests are viewed as obstacles to progress. As a result, forests in these countries are being cut down at an incredible rate. And because of the special soil and climatic conditions in these areas, the cleared forests often can't regenerate.

Much of this *deforestation* is occurring in the rain forests of the tropics. The reasons tropical rain forests are being cut down vary. A lot of tropical forestland is cut down by subsistence farmers, who farm the land for a couple of years and then are forced to move on after the land has lost its productivity. Huge tracts of rain forest are also cleared by cattle ranchers, who convert the land to pasture.

Scientists aren't sure what the environmental consequences of tropical deforestation will be, but many think that it could seriously affect the earth's climate. Others point out that, by destroying these forests, we're losing a huge potential source of medicines, foods, and other products that benefit people. And of course, when the rain forests go, the incredible diversity of plants and animals that they harbor will also be destroyed. (Scientists think there are thousands of rain forest plants and animals that we don't even know about yet.)

Obviously, ethical and sensible forestry practices need to be developed and implemented in rain forests. Without careful management, these forests could slip away before we even know what we've lost. (For more about tropical rain forests and the problem of deforestation, see the activity on page 52.)

Some scientists estimate that 1100 acres (440 ha) of tropical rain forest in South and Central America are cleared every hour. In the past century, the world's total acreage of tropical rain forest has been cut in half.

We All Need Forests

Objectives:
List five ways forest lands are used. Discuss competition between forest uses.

Ages:
Primary and Intermediate

Materials:
- *copies of page 59*
- *chalkboard or easel paper*
- *tree collage materials*
- *pictures from magazines and newspapers*
- *glue or tape*
- *cardboard*

Subjects:
Science and Social Studies

Leonard Lee Rue II

flying squirrel

What would you do if you were in charge of 20,000 acres (8000 ha) of forest? If you owned a paper company, you would probably plant a species of fast-growing pine or other "paper tree" and manage as much of the forest as you could for pulpwood. If you were a wildlife biologist, you would try to manage the forest in a way that would provide the best habitat for the different species of wildlife you wanted to protect. And if you were a recreation planner, you might manage the forest to provide good campsites, hiking trails, ski paths, fishing streams, bike paths, and wildlife study areas.

Although most people don't realize it, most of the forests in this country are managed. *How* a forest is managed depends on what it will be used for. In the past, most forests were managed for only one type of use, such as for raising pulpwood trees. But today, many more are being managed for several different uses at a time through the practice of *multiple use management.*

In this activity, your group will get a chance to discuss different forest uses and how some of these uses compete. They will also learn why multiple use management is so important.

Start off the activity by asking your group to name ways that they or their families use forests. (for hiking, birding, hunting, fishing, camping, and so on) List the uses the children come up with on the chalkboard or a large sheet of easel paper. Then explain that forests are also important because they provide habitat for many types of wildlife and contain important natural resources. Next ask if someone can define the word *manage.* Explain that in order for people to use forests in different ways, forest managers must manage forests in different ways.

Next pass out copies of page 59. Tell the children that this page lists some of the things that many forests are managed for. Ask them to look at the three rows on the page. Starting with the first row, labeled *wildlife,* discuss some of the ways forests

are managed to help protect different species of wildlife. Use this background information to explain how forests are managed for wildlife:

Saving Snags: One way people manage for wildlife in a forest is by leaving dead trees, or *snags,* standing instead of cutting them down. Snags provide nesting cavities for many birds and mammals, such as owls, woodpeckers, wood ducks, bluebirds, raccoons, and squirrels.

Building Brushpiles: By building brushpiles in a forest and along forest edges, forest managers help provide hiding and nesting sites for many animals that live on the ground, such as foxes, rabbits, wood thrushes, and chipmunks.

Letting Logs Lie: Many types of animals use logs for nesting and hiding places. By not removing logs, managers can help provide homes and feeding areas for many kinds of wildlife.

Building Feeders and Nesting Boxes: Putting up nesting boxes in forests that have limited nesting sites can help attract wildlife. So can setting up feeding stations for birds and mammals.

Burning: For some species, the only way to maintain the right kind of habitat is to burn the area on a regular basis to get rid of undergrowth.

Picking the Right Plants: By planting certain types of trees and shrubs in a forest area, wildlife managers can provide habitat for specific types of wildlife.

Now have the kids look at the row labeled *recreation.* Compare this list with the list the children came up with. Discuss the fact that the forest is an important place for people to relax, enjoy nature, and exercise.

Explain that some of the ways people use forests for recreation compete with the needs of wildlife and can also disrupt the plants that grow there. For example, to build ski slopes in a forest, heavy equipment must come in and cut down trees to make the runs. Roads and parking lots must be built so that people can get to the slopes and park. Many times ski lodges and other facilities are also built. And once the ski slopes are open to the public, lots of people will probably use them. All these changes will affect the wildlife in the area. For example, many animal nesting sites might be destroyed or disrupted; the soil in many areas could get packed down and become eroded; and littering would most likely increase.

Ask the children if they can think of other ways recreational uses of the forest can harm the wildlife. Then explain that the role of many forest managers is to balance the uses of a forest so that wildlife can be protected and people can use it for recreation.

Finally have the kids look at the row labeled *products*. Explain that forests are also used for commercial purposes. Some forest areas are managed for lumber, some are managed for pulpwood, and some are opened up for oil, gas, and mineral exploration. Discuss how these uses can disrupt the forest community and compete with wildlife and recreational uses. For example, you probably wouldn't want to camp near a strip mine in a forest or hike along an area that is being lumbered. Ask the children why it is important to have commercial uses in a forest. (People need forest products.)

Now explain that because of all these forest uses, forest managers should try to make well-informed decisions about how best to manage forests while satisfying competing uses. In many national forests, for example, commercial foresters, wildlife biologists, recreation planners, soil scientists, and many other experts will consult with each other to work out the best management plan. That can mean coming up with the most efficient way to grow pulpwood or timber trees while doing the least harm to the forest community; providing for recreational facilities in some parts of the forest; and managing for specific types of wildlife throughout the forest. By using multiple use management, forests can be used productively and satisfy many needs.

After discussing forest management, have the kids make forest collages showing all the different uses of a forest. They can cut pictures from magazines, draw their own pictures, and tape or glue on pieces of real forest items, such as toothpicks, paper, seeds, and roots. Have each person write a short paragraph explaining his or her collage, then hang the collages around the room.

Disappearing Trees

Listen to and discuss a make-believe story about a forest that is destroyed; then read an article about the problem facing South America's rain forests.

Objectives:
Define deforestation. List three competing uses of trees. Discuss the deforestation problems in South America.

Ages:
Primary, Intermediate, and Advanced

Materials:
● *copies of pages 60 and 61*

(continued next page)

I n many parts of the world forests are quickly disappearing. In some countries they are disappearing because thousands of trees are cut down each year for firewood. In other areas forests are harvested for timber or are cut down to clear the land for farming or cattle grazing. And as populations grow and cities spread in many countries, forests are cleared to make way for roads, houses, schools, shopping centers, and so on.

As we mentioned in the background information on page 50, some countries are now managing their forests. But in many other areas forest management is not practiced—and the trees in these areas are in trouble.

In this two-part activity your group can begin to learn about tropical deforestation—what it is, why it is occurring, how it affects people, land, and wildlife, and what can be done to help slow it down. (Only the first part of this activity is suitable for primary groups. Adapt the suggested discussion questions to fit the level of your group.)

- *copy of* The Lorax *by Dr. Seuss*
- *chalkboard or easel paper*
- *209-foot (62-m) piece of twine*
- *pictures of plants and animals that live in rain forests of the world (see the bibliography on page 75)*

Subjects:
Social Studies and Science

PART 1: LEARNING FROM "THE LORAX"

For this part of the activity you will need to get a copy of *The Lorax* by Dr. Seuss (Random House, 1971), which you can find in most libraries and bookstores. *The Lorax* is a make-believe story about what happened to a forest when people didn't use it wisely.

Read *The Lorax* to your group and discuss what happens in the story. Ask the children if they think the story is trying to teach a lesson, and if so, what the lesson is. Ask them how they feel about the Lorax and the Once-ler. Then ask them to think about their own community and how they would feel if all the trees in a nearby park were cut down. What would happen to the wildlife? What would they miss most if the park were no longer there?

Now take a vote. Ask how many of the kids think trees should never be cut down. Have the children explain why they voted the way they did. Then have the group name some of the ways people use trees. (Make a list on the chalkboard or on a large piece of easel paper.) Add other uses the children might not have known about or thought of. (See "From Paper to Plastic" on page 65 for ideas.) Explain that trees are important to us in many ways. We enjoy their beauty when we go hiking and camping, we sit under them for shade, we breathe the oxygen they give off during photosynthesis, and we climb them for fun. Trees are also important to wildlife. But if we never cut down trees, we would not have many of the products we use every day, such as wooden furniture, paper, some plastics, and many other tree products.

Next ask the kids if they think the people in the story needed thneeds in the first place. Do they think it was worth cutting down the truffula trees to make thneeds? Ask why the Once-ler kept making so many thneeds.

Now ask if anyone has any ideas about what the Once-ler could have done so that he could have made thneeds, but still not permanently harmed the forest. (He could have cut down only some of the trees, replanted a tree each time he cut one, and so on.) Discuss the things that the children came up with and then talk about how forests in our country are managed today so that they can be used in many different ways (see pages 48 and 49). Explain that trees are considered a *renewable resource,* but they must be taken care of and managed well so that they don't disappear. (Unlike non-renewable resouces, such as oil, coal, natural gas, some minerals, and other things that can't be replenished, trees can be replanted and won't "run out" if they are well managed.)

Now have the kids vote again on whether or not trees should ever be cut. Did anyone change his or her mind?

(continued next page)

Once you've talked about *The Lorax* and discussed why it is important to manage trees and plan for the future, introduce your group to a worldwide forest problem—the destruction of tropical rain forests. First ask if someone can say where most of the tropical rain forests in the world are located. (Tropical rain forests grow near the equator in parts of Asia, Africa, Australia, and Central and South America. The areas where they grow have warm temperatures all year and a continuous growing season.) Point out where they grow on a map of the world. Then explain that many tropical rain forests are in trouble because people are cutting them down much faster than they can regrow.

Now point to the Amazon River Basin. Explain that some of the largest tracts of tropical rain forest in the world are found here. (This area includes the Amazon River and the drainage areas of all rivers flowing into the Amazon.) The area of rain forest found along the Amazon is called Amazonia. It covers an area about the size of the United States east of the Rocky Mountains. (Most, but not all, of Amazonia is in Brazil.)

Ask the children if they can name some of the plants and animals that live in tropical rain forests. (parrots, monkeys, orchids, snakes, lizards, sloths, and so on) Show the children some pictures of rain forests and plants and animals that live in them. Explain that some scientists think that Amazonia is the richest natural community in the world. And many parts have not even been studied yet!

Now write the word *deforestation* on the board and ask if someone can explain what it means. (An area that's been deforested has had its forest cleared away.) Explain that thousands of acres of rain forest in Amazonia are being cut down every day. (Tropical rain forests in other parts of the world are also being cut down, but this activity will focus mainly on Amazonia.) And just as the Lorax was concerned about the loss of truffula trees, so are many people concerned about tropical deforestation. Point out that if

tropical deforestation isn't slowed or stopped, huge tracts of rain forests and all the wildlife in them will disappear forever.

To help your group visualize how much forest is being cleared in Amazonia, take them outside to measure an acre (.4 ha). Explain that over 19 acres (7.6 ha) of rain forest are being cleared each minute in Central and South America—that's about 1100 acres (440 ha) each hour. Using a 209-foot (62-m) piece of twine, have the kids help "build" an acre. Start with one side of the square (have one person stand at the start and another take the twine and stand 209 feet away) and then use the twine to measure another side, continuing until you have a square with kids standing in each of its corners. (This area is approximately the size of an acre.)

Now bring the group back inside and pass out a copy of the article on pages 60 and 61. It will help the kids understand some of the reasons that the rain forests in many parts of South America are being cleared. (Tell the children that tropical deforestation is also a problem in many other parts of the world, including Central America, Southeast Asia, and Africa.)

After everyone has read the article, talk about the problems in Amazonia. Make a list of the reasons that the rain forest is so important. Here are a few to get you started:

- Rain forests contain half of all the known species of plants and animals in the world.
- The trees in rain forests help hold the soil in place and help hold water for entire regions. Without the rain forest, many scientists think that drought, flooding, and other natural catastrophes would increase.
- Many species of migratory birds winter in tropical rain forests.
- Many of the plants and animals of rain forests have never been seen or studied. Scientists think there are thousands of species that we may never know about if rain forests disappear.
- We get many drugs and medicines from plants that grow in the tropics. Since many rain forest plants have not

even been studied, there are probably many more medical discoveries waiting to be found.

- The rain forests of the world are beautiful and fascinating. If we lost them, we would lose some of the unique natural areas in the world.

Next make a list of the ways people use the land and the timber in rain forests. (to graze cattle; to farm; to harvest timber for buildings, furniture, paper, and other tree products; as building sites for houses, schools, and roads; to plant fruit, coffee, and drugs [cocaine and marijuana], and so on) Ask the children if they can think of anything that could help stop the deforestation. Then discuss some of the things people around the world are doing to help solve the tropical deforestation problem.

Here are some ideas:

- **Be Aware of Tropical Wood:** Much of the wood that is harvested from tropical rain forests around the world, such as teak, mahogany, rosewood, and lauan, is sold in the United States. Many conservation organizations think that some tropical wood and wood products should not be allowed into our country. Instead, they say people should buy products made of native woods, such as pine, oak, and maple.

- **Don't Support Tropical Pet Trade:** Many groups also suggest that people avoid buying exotic pets that come from rain forest areas, such as parrots, turtles, fish, and snakes, as well as products made from tropical animals (snakeskin accessories, furs, feather jewelry, and other products). If people don't support rain forest trade, some of the destruction might be discouraged.

- **Support Conservation Organizations:** Many people are donating money to organizations that are trying to help conserve the tropics, such as the World Wildlife Fund, the Nature Conservancy, and the National Wildlife Federation.

- **Write Letters:** Many people are also writing letters to industries and other organizations, such as the World Bank, that are helping to finance many of the cattle ranching and road building operations in South America. They're asking these organizations to stop funding projects that harm tropical rain forests.

- **Learn More About the Tropics:** Many people think that one of the most important things everyone can do is to learn more about the wildlife and vegetation of rain forests to help convince others that it is important not to lose these unique areas.

toucan

(continued next page)

- **Support Population Control:** In many tropical rain forest areas, human populations are growing so fast that the resources are strained. To help people in overpopulated areas learn about birth control and the problems of over-population, many people are donating money to international population control agencies.

As a wrap-up, explain that many scientists around the world are trying to help countries in Central and South America (as well as in other parts of the world) learn how to manage their rain forests in a way that will protect the animals and plants in them, while still providing for the needs of the people who live there. Some of the things they are suggesting that the governments and companies in these countries do are to:

—set aside certain areas as national parks to protect plants and animals that are in immediate danger
—teach farmers to farm without destroying huge tracts of forests; help farmers

increase their yields by teaching them how to enrich the soil, prevent soil erosion, protect their crops from pests with ecologically safe methods, and plant crops among native plants
—learn how to reforest areas in the rain forest that have been destroyed
—encourage scientific research to learn more about the ecology of rain forests
—restrict cattle ranching and slash-and-burn farming to areas that are the least fragile
—plant native tree crops such as coffee and cacao, instead of non-native crops that do more harm to the soil
—protect the native cultures that have used rain forests for hundreds of years without permanently harming them and learn how they live in harmony with the rain forests
—limit clear-cutting as much as possible and rely more on selective harvesting
—plant crops that provide food for many years, such as fruit and nut trees, so the land does not have to be plowed under each year

Tree Champs

Measure trees and hold a contest to find the biggest tree in town.

Objectives:
Explain how champion trees are determined. Define height, circumference, *and* crown spread *and measure them on a tree.*

Ages:
Intermediate and Advanced

Materials:
- *tape measures (one per team)*
- *paper and pencils*
- *yardsticks (one per team)*
- *tree field guides*

Subjects:
Science and Math

Standing 275 feet (82.5 m) high and measuring more than 80 feet (24 m) in circumference, the biggest giant sequoia in California is also the biggest tree in the United States. It is one of more than 650 "champion trees" in the nation. But even though all champion trees are considered "giants," several are less than 20 feet (6 m) high.

In this activity your kids can learn what it takes for a tree to be designated a champion. They can also learn some of the techniques used to measure trees. And afterward they'll be able to size up some trees on their own.

First explain to the kids that to be considered a champion a tree must be the biggest of its kind. A special formula is used to determine just how large a tree is. First the tree's height, circumference, and

average crown spread (spread of its branches) must be measured. Then the measurements are plugged into this formula: *height + circumference + ¼ crown = point total*. The tree of a particular species that has the most "points" (greatest sum) is considered the champion. (If a tree comes within 5 points of the champion, the two trees are listed as co-champions. And if a tree is close, but not quite big enough to "tie" or "beat" the champion, it is put on a special list of "challenger trees.")

All of the champion trees are listed in the *National Register of Big Trees*, maintained by the American Forestry Association. And because a lot of people keep searching for bigger trees and the registered champions sometimes lose points (get struck by lightning and lose a branch, for example) the list is constantly changing.

Distance A should be the same as distance B.

MEASURING UP

Now tell the kids that they're going to measure some trees and then, on their own time, find the biggest tree in the neighborhood. Divide the group into teams of four and give each team a measuring tape and a yardstick. Then take the kids outside and have each team pick a tree to measure. Explain that the tree they pick does not have to be the biggest one they can find—they are measuring this first tree for practice and later will try to find the biggest one in the neighborhood. As they measure the trees, have the kids write down their measurements and then record where their tree is located and what kind of tree it is. (They can use field guides to help them identify the trees.) Here's how the kids should measure their trees:

Circumference: The circumference of a tree is the distance around its trunk. It is usually measured 4½ feet (1.4 m) from the ground and is approximated to the nearest inch (2.5 cm). To measure the circumference, have one person hold one end of the measuring tape against the tree, 4½ feet off the ground. Another child can wrap the tape around the trunk.

If the kids aren't tall enough to measure the circumference at 4½ feet or if there are branches at the 4½-foot mark, have them measure at the thinnest point below the mark.

Height: The height of a tree is measured from the ground to its top twig and is approximated to the nearest foot (30 cm). Have a couple of the kids in each team stay on *level* ground as they follow these directions to measure their tree's height:

1. Hold your arm out in front of you so that your fist is at eye level. (Your arm shouldn't be bent at all.) Have another team member measure the distance from your fist to your eye (see line A on diagram).

2. Face the tree you want to measure and hold a yardstick so that the distance from your hand to the top of the stick is the same as the distance you measured in step 1 (see line B on diagram). Make sure you hold the stick straight up and down and not at an angle.

3. Walk backward away from the tree until you can see the base of the tree by looking over your fist, and the top of the tree by looking over the top of the yardstick. (Don't move anything but your eyes. See diagram.)

4. When you can see the tree completely by sighting over the top of the yardstick and the top of your fist, have the other team members measure the distance between you and the tree. This distance is the approximate height of the tree. *(continued next page)*

Crown Spread: The crown spread of a tree is the distance its branches spread away from its trunk. It's approximated to the nearest foot (30 cm) and is usually taken as an average.

To measure the average crown spread of the tree first have the kids find the branch that sticks out farthest from the trunk. Have one child stand directly under its tip; then have another child go to the opposite side of the tree. He or she should stand directly under the tip of the branch that sticks out farthest on that side. Tell these two team members to take one or two steps to the side of the trunk, then have the other team members measure the distance between them (see diagram).

Now have the kids find the shortest branch of the crown. Have one child stand directly under its tip while another child goes to the opposite side of the tree and finds the shortest branch of the crown on that side. Again, have the other team members measure the distance between these two children. Finally, to get the average crown spread, have the kids add the two distances together and divide by two.

Here's some sample data you can show the kids:
Height: 60 feet
Circumference: 32 inches
Crown Spread:
 widest point: 28 feet
 narrowest point: 20 feet
 average crown spread: 24 feet
Point total: $60 + 32 + \frac{1}{4}(24) = 98$

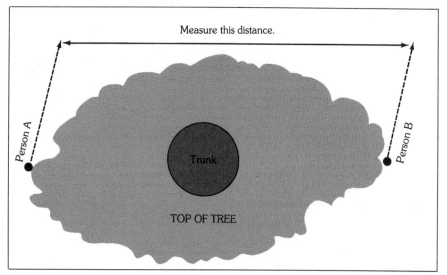

Measure this distance.

Person A

Person B

Trunk

TOP OF TREE

THE NEIGHBORHOOD CHAMP

Now that the kids can measure trees, try holding a contest to see which team can find the biggest tree around. Be sure to give the kids plenty of time to find and measure some trees on their own time, and tell them to write down where their tree is located, what kind of tree it is, and the tree's height, circumference, and crown spread measurements. They should also use the champion tree formula to find out the total number of points their trees scored. Afterward, each team can compare their "winners" to those the other teams found. Which team found the biggest tree?

As a variation, try putting together your own town register of big trees. Just give each team three different species of trees to locate and measure and have them look for the biggest specimens in the area. Then list these local champions alphabetically, writing each tree's circumference, height, average crown spread, and total points next to its name.

You might also want to find out what your state's official tree is and have the kids try to find the biggest state tree in town.

CopycatPage We All Need Forests

WILDLIFE

nesting boxes

brushpiles

logs

snags

feeders

RECREATION

hiking

camping

fishing

skiing

PRODUCTS

paper

ICE CREAM   MILK

lumber

charcoal

gas and oil

The largest reptile in the world lives there. So does the largest insect. In an average square four-mile (10.4-km) plot, you can find over 400 species of birds! Some scientists say there may be as many as thirty million or more species of insects living there—more than all other species of animals put together. Over two thousand species of fish live in its waters—that's eight times as many as live in the Mississippi. And in some two-acre (.8-ha) plots there are over 160 different species of trees—compared to an average of eight per acre in our country. What is this amazing place? It's called Amazonia and it's located in South America in the Amazon River valley. Amazonia is the largest tract of tropical rain forest left in the world.

But things are not going well in Amazonia. The rain forest there is being cleared faster than most people realize. Each year, an area the size of Maryland is chopped down. And the deforestation hasn't slowed. Why is the rain forest disappearing? The problem is very complicated, but here are three of the main causes for the deforestation:

1 Farming: Many of the people in South America are poor. To grow enough food to survive, they turn rain forest land into farmland. To clear the rain forest they use a practice called *slash-and-burn*. This means they cut down the trees in a small area and then burn the area to get rid of fallen trees and other vegetation. They plant crops on the land, but soon have to move on to a new area because the soil wears out. (Tropical rain forest soil is not very rich. When an animal or plant dies it decomposes very quickly in the heat and humidity. The nutrients from the dead plants and animals are immediately used by other plants instead of staying in the soil. That means that when the trees are cleared away, most of the nutrients disappear too.)

2 Timbering: Many lumber companies also harm the rain forest. They harvest the tropical trees and sell the timber to the United States, Japan, and other countries. These companies damage the forest by cutting down trees and also by building logging roads and using heavy equipment, which can hurt the soil and wildlife. (This is more of a problem in the tropical rain forests of Southeast Asia and Africa than it is in Amazonia.)

The forests are also cleared for firewood and charcoal. Many people that live in rain forest areas depend entirely on wood (and charcoal) to cook with and to heat their homes.

3 Cattle Grazing: Much of the rain forest in South and Central America is cleared away to make pastures for beef cattle. After clearing the land, cattle companies plant grass and raise large herds of cattle. Since the rain forest soil is not rich, it cannot support grazing for very long. And in five to ten years, when grass will no longer grow, the ranchers have to move on and clear new land. This overgrazed land becomes useless—nothing can grow because all the minerals have been washed away and the soil has been packed down by the cattle.

*I*n the time it takes you to read this article, hundreds of trees will have been cut down. And unlike the trees growing in this country, the trees in the rain forests of South America cannot regrow easily.

With over one million trees being cut down every day, many scientists are worried that much of Amazonia's forests, as well as forests in Central America, Southeast Asia, and Africa, may be gone in less than 75 years. And if they go, millions of species of animals and other plants will disappear too. Scientists also think the disappearing rain forests will create a lot of other problems, including changes in weather patterns around the world and changes in other natural communities in South America.

Think about what you would miss most if there were no more rain forests. Besides all the troubles it could cause in the world, there would be no more colorful toucans, slow-moving sloths, or enormous anacondas. Many of our migrating songbirds would no longer have a home. And gliding lizards, huge air plants, and species we've never even seen would vanish. And the world would never be the same.

TREES IN OUR LIVES

People and trees go way back . . . sharing a history that started millions of years ago. Even before ancient civilizations sprang up along river valleys, small communities of hunters and gatherers depended on trees for food, shelter, and fuel. As hunting-gathering skills turned into farming skills, people began to clear small patches of forests with primitive stone axes. They planted grains and used the wood from the fallen trees for fuel and shelter.

It wasn't until civilizations started spreading along the great river valleys, such as the Nile, Tigris, Indus, Yangtze, and Euphrates, that the forests first began to disappear. Since most hardy timber trees do not grow along river floodplains, the people living there had to exploit other areas to get the wood they needed. The ancient Egyptians who lived in the Nile Valley, for example, harvested thousands of cedars from the forested mountains in Lebanon. They used the wood to build houses, palaces, temples, and ships. They also made wooden rollers to move enormous stones needed to build the pyramids. In a short time, the cedars became scarce and the Egyptians had to look elsewhere for timber.

CHARCOAL, SMELTING, AND DRUIDS

As civilizations grew, so did the demand for wood and wood products. When smelting (heating metal ores to high temperatures to get pure metal) was invented, charcoal became a "hot" item because it was used to fuel the forges. (Charcoal, which makes fires burn very hot, is wood that has been partially burned in a special process.) Copper, bronze, and iron were all made in ancient charcoal-fired forges or furnaces.

These metals—especially iron—had a big influence on the forests of the world. Iron axes were strong and kept a sharp edge longer than stone axes and helped clear forests easily. The Celts of Europe and other ancient civilizations used iron tools as well as many wood products. In fact, trees were so important in so many ways that many cultures worshipped trees and held special tree ceremonies. For example, Celtic priests, called *druids,* thought oaks possessed magical powers. These priests often held their religious ceremonies in oak groves.

TREES DURING THE MIDDLE AGES

By the Middle Ages, wood and other tree products were part of everyday life. Wood was used to build houses, boats, tools, carts, wine presses, and furniture. Peasants fattened their hogs on acorns (called mast) and kept special "bee trees" for honey. Many people also gathered tree nuts, fruit, and bark for food and medicine. Wood ash was another important tree by-product, and was used to make glass and soap. And charcoal continued to be essential for forging iron and also for brewing beer.

With trees providing all the fuel and building material, as well as filling many other needs, many forests became seriously depleted. In France, for example, there was less forested land in the 1300s than there is today. In some areas, wood became so scarce that wooden coffins had to be reused.

During these times, when forests were dwindling, many people began the practice of *coppicing.* (A tree that has been coppiced is one which, after it's been cut

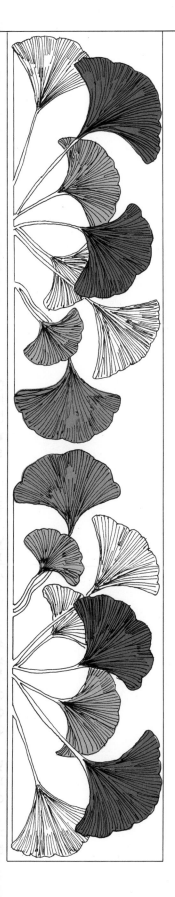

sends up shoots from its stump. Many, but not all, types of trees can "grow back" this way.) When a forest was cleared, the shoots from the old stumps were left to grow for 7 to 20 years, and the skinny saplings were then chopped down and used to make charcoal, building materials, and other products. The stumps continued to regenerate coppiced forests for many generations. (Coppicing is still used as a management tool today.)

By the end of the Middle Ages, lords, bishops, dukes, and other high-ranking members of society owned most of the forests in Europe. These aristocrats often maintained their forests as hunting preserves and allowed peasant farmers, herders, and other "common" people to use only certain areas in the preserve at certain times.

TREES AFTER THE MIDDLE AGES

During the Renaissance, trees were valued not only for their wood, but also for their aesthetic qualities. Many of the great Renaissance painters, writers, and musicians were inspired by nature and the great forests of the world. During this time, many wooden musical instruments were invented, such as the harpsichord, guitar, and violin.

By the end of the 17th century, trees were as valuable to the nations of the world as oil is today. One of the major uses of wood during this time was for shipbuilding. Warring nations needed tall, sturdy timber to build their huge warships. After much of Europe began to run out of good ship timber, forests in Africa, New Zealand, Australia, and North America were exploited.

The 18th century brought great increases in the use of wood—especially when the Industrial Revolution took off. In fact, the forests of the world could not keep up with the demands for wood. The need for charcoal to fuel iron forges was one of the main culprits. But even after coal replaced charcoal as the chief fuel for smelting, the demand for wood and wood products continued to soar.

By the end of the 18th century, many European nations began to manage their forests to help protect them. They began to set aside certain areas for recreation and other areas for lumbering. (See page 48 for information about multiple use forests.)

But in North America, early settlers viewed the vast forests as obstacles to be chopped down so the land could be farmed and settlements could move west. During the westward expansion, more and more trees "got the ax."

WORKING ON THE RAILROAD

The 19th century brought a new use of wood to North America and other parts of the world—the building of the railroad. Although iron and steel were used to build the engines and rails, huge amounts of wood were needed for railroad platforms and crossties that supported the rails. In America, railroads replaced the covered wagon, speeding the settlement of the West. In Brazil, India, and other countries, trains opened up virgin forests, making tropical timber and other tree products, such as rubber and cocoa, widely available for the first time.

As the railroad opened up the world, people became more educated and better-traveled, and there was an increased demand for books, newspapers, magazines, and other printed material. Pulpwood from trees replaced rags as the main ingredient in paper, which speeded up the paper-making process and made it much cheaper. (Many centuries earlier, the Chinese had invented paper, using the shredded bark of the mulberry tree and mixing it with scraps of linen and hemp. The Mayans also made paper, using bark from the fig tree. Up until the 19th century though, most paper was made from linen or rags.)

TREES IN OUR LIVES TODAY

As the paper and lumber industry boomed in the late 1800s and early 1900s, many people became concerned about the world's dwindling forests—especially the disappearance of huge tracts of wilderness. Since then, thousands of acres of forests have been set aside as national parks, forests, and preserves around the world. Although many of these forests are multiple use forests that allow timbering, mining, grazing, recreation, and other uses, many are protected as wilderness areas. These "wild" forests are left alone—to grow naturally as all forests once did.

Today, most of us never stop to think about the many ways trees fit into our lives. We use wood to build houses, schools, chairs, tables, and all kinds of other things. We also get many foods, medicines, cosmetics, and plastics from trees or tree derivatives (see page 65). And tree energy, in the form of methanol and other potential fuels extracted from wood, is becoming more important as oil products become expensive and scarce.

Many of us also never stop to think about the consequences of "no more wilderness" or what will happen if we keep losing 1100 acres (440 ha) of rain forest in Central and South America every hour, day after day and year after year. But as populations around the world increase, the demand for more wood, more farmland, and more tree by-products will continue to grow. And that means everyone needs to take a closer look at what trees mean to us. After sharing such a long history with trees, we owe it to ourselves—and to the forests of the world—not to take trees for granted.

Bruce Norfleet

From Paper to Plastic

Discover some of the many ways people use trees.

Objectives:
Name 10 products that we get from trees. Talk about how some of these products are made.

Ages:
Primary and Intermediate

Materials:
- *copies of page 70*
- *pencils*
- *crayons or markers*

Subject:
Science

 t's hard to imagine what life would be like without trees—we use them to make everything from cardboard to chewing gum. In this activity your kids can discover just how big a role trees play in their everyday lives.

First pass out a copy of page 70 to each person. Tell the kids that there are more than 40 things in the picture that are made, in some way, from trees. Then have them use a pencil to circle all of the "tree objects" they can find. Afterward, go over their answers using the information below. Then let the kids color the picture.

PUTTING TREES TO WORK

Building with Wood:

People build a lot of different things with wood. When logs are brought to the sawmill their bark is removed and they are carefully measured and cut into lumber. Most lumber is used to construct houses and other buildings. But some is used to make athletic equipment, crates, furniture, tool handles, wooden toys, works of art, and many other things.

Wood products in the picture: banister, baseball bat, blocks, bookshelf, broom handle, bulletin board frame, cabinets, chairs, clock, counter, door, fence (seen through open door), fruit bowl, molding (on walls), paintbrush handle, picture frames, sofa, stairs, stereo cabinet and speakers, spools for thread, stools, tables, tennis racket, umbrella handle, window frame, wood inside walls

Making Paper:

Paper is made from cellulose, the major component of cell walls in most plants. And most paper in the United States is made with cellulose that comes from trees. To turn a tree into paper, the bark is first stripped off and the trunk is chopped into small pieces, or *chips*. Afterward the chips are usually cooked with chemicals until they form an oatmeal-like pulp.

Next the pulp is washed and the impurities (such as dirt) are filtered out, leaving a pulp of cellulose fibers and water. This "clean" pulp is then sent through a series of machines where the fibers are flattened and broken apart so that they will form a smooth sheet when the paper is dried.

Eventually the pulp is run onto screens and the water is drained off. And finally, the newly made paper is compressed and dried. (Depending upon the chemical process used to make the pulp and the amount of refining the pulp goes through, different kinds of paper can be made, such as coffee filter paper, heavy writing paper, and so on.)

Paper products in the picture: books, candy wrapper, cereal box, gift (wrapping and box), magazines, milk container, newspaper, notes on bulletin board, paper towels, record album covers

Cellulose Is Everywhere:

Besides being used to make paper, cellulose is also one of the ingredients of many other products. For example, it can be mixed with certain chemicals, turned into a thick liquid, and then squeezed through small holes or slits to form fibers. The fibers can be used to make carpeting or conveyor belts, or they might be spun into fabric (rayon and some others) for making clothes or furniture. Different kinds of plastic films, such as cellophane and photographic film, are also made from cellulose.

Cellulose is also added to certain substances that are used to make car steering wheels, toothbrush handles, Ping-Pong balls, and some other plastic products. And depending on how it's processed, cellulose can be used in making explosives, thickeners in shampoo and salad dressing, and wallpaper paste.

Cellulose products in the picture: buttons, comb, curtains, eyeglasses frame, hair-

(continued next page)

brush handle, luggage, pillows, rug, upholstery on sofa

About Bark:

Tree bark has a lot of different uses. For example, the spongy bark of the cork oak tree, which grows in the Mediterranean countries of Europe and Africa, is stripped off and made into bottle cap liners, bottle stoppers, floats, and even heat shields for space vehicles.

Special chemicals in the bark of some trees also have a lot of different uses. For example, some trees produce *tannin*, which is used to cure leather.
Bark products in the picture: baseball (has a cork center), bulletin board

Using the Ooze:

Some trees ooze special saps called gums and resins. Gums and resins can be used to make many things, including cosmetics, mouthwash, paint thinner, perfumes, soap, and coatings for vitamins and other pills. Other trees produce a special juice called latex that can be used to make conveyor belts, hoses, rubber tires, and other rubber products.
Gum, resin, and rubber products in the picture: paint, rubber gloves

Eating Tree Food:

People eat the fruit, nuts, roots, and bark of many different trees. Most fruit and nuts can be eaten right off of the tree. But other tree "parts" must be cooked, dried, or processed in some way before people can eat them. (For more about food from trees, see "Tree Treats" below.)
Tree foods in the picture: apples, chocolate bar (cacao tree beans are used to make chocolate), orange

Besides the products we've listed, trees can also be used in making adhesives, asphalt, baby food, cleaners, inks, medicines, and pesticides. And many trees are sources of natural fibers that can be made into clothes, furniture, and stuffing material for cushions and life jackets.

Tree Treats

Research a tree food and then sample some tree snacks.

Objectives:
Describe three foods that come from trees. Talk about the trees they come from.

Ages:
Primary, Intermediate, and Advanced

Materials:
- *reference books*
- *slips of paper*
- *plates (optional)*
- *forks (optional)*
- *ingredients and utensils for making tree snacks (optional—see individual recipes)*

Subject:
Science

I t's amazing how many foods we get from trees. We eat tree fruit, nuts, sap, roots, shoots, and sometimes even tree bark. In this activity your kids can learn a little more about different tree foods and then present what they have learned during a "tree treats" celebration.

To get started, write each of the following words on a slip of paper:

allspice	lemons
almonds	limes
apples	mangos
apricots	maple syrup
avocados	nectarines
cacao	nutmeg
cashews	olives
cherries	oranges
chestnuts	peaches
cinnamon	pears
cloves	pecans
coconuts	persimmons
dates	pistachios
figs	prunes
grapefruit	walnuts

Have everyone pick one of the slips out of a hat, then explain that the fruit, nut, seed, or spice on each person's slip is a kind of food that comes from a tree. Tell the kids that they'll be given some time to research their tree foods and the trees the foods come from. Then, on Tree Treats Day, everyone can present what they have learned.

Here are a few ideas for the kind of information the kids could include in their talks:
- what kind of tree the food comes from
- where the tree grew originally and where it grows today
- how the tree food is used (cooked, eaten raw, or both and the kinds of products it's used in or made into)
- any interesting facts about the food (its history, famous people who used it or cultivated it, and so on)

The kids' presentations can also include posters, displays, samples of the foods themselves, or any other props they can come up with. For example, the person who picks the slip with the word *nutmeg* on it could draw a poster showing the islands on which the nutmeg tree originated (the Spice Islands). The person who picks cacao (the tree from which we get chocolate) could put together a display showing different kinds of chocolate products, such as baking chocolate, milk chocolate, semi-sweet chocolate, cocoa mix, cocoa butter, and so on. And the person who draws the apple slip could bring in slices of Delicious, Granny Smith, McIntosh, or other apple varieties for the kids to try.

On the day of the celebration, you can bring in fruit, nuts, orange juice, apple juice, and other tree foods for the kids to munch on. You might also want to put together a few special tree treats for the kids. Here are two recipes you can try. (The words in italics are the ingredients that come from trees. You may want to name these tree foods when you serve the treats to the kids.)

Bruce Norfleet

Fruit 'n' Nut Spread

(Makes enough spread for a group of about 25 people.)
8-oz package cream cheese, softened
1½ cups non-dairy whipped topping
1 cup finely chopped *apple*
1 cup chopped *walnuts*
½ cup chopped *dates*
2 large cans *peach* halves
2 large cans *pear* halves

Combine cream cheese and non-dairy whipped topping in a large bowl. Add apple, walnuts, and dates. Stir until well mixed. Spoon into depressions in peach or pear halves and serve.

Tree Balls

(Makes three to four dozen balls.)
1 cup dried *apricots*
1 cup dried *figs*
1 cup dried, pitted *prunes*
⅔ cup *almonds*
1 small package shredded *coconut*
½ teaspoon ground *cloves*
1 teaspoon *cinnamon*

Grind the apricots, figs, prunes, and almonds together into tiny bits in a food grinder or food processor. Stir in the spices. Mold the mixture into little balls and then roll the balls in the shredded coconut.

Celebrate Trees!

Participate in a week of tree activities.

Objectives:
Describe several ways trees are important in our lives. Explain why people celebrate Arbor Day.

Ages:
Primary, Intermediate, and Advanced

Materials:
See suggested activities for ideas.

Subjects:
Science, History, Social Studies, and Creative Writing

Bruce Norfleet

Arbor Day is a special day when people learn about, plant, and care for trees. The first Arbor Day celebration took place in Nebraska on April 10, 1872. Today, all fifty states and many Canadian provinces celebrate Arbor Day. (The date varies from state to state and province to province.) Other countries around the world also hold special tree celebrations. Here are some ideas you can try during the week of Arbor Day or anytime to help your group learn more about how they can take care of trees and conserve forest resources. We've also listed a few suggestions for some creative ways your kids can celebrate trees and Arbor Day.

- Discuss why trees are considered a *renewable resource*. Then explain why it is important to manage trees. (See "Learning from The Lorax" on page 53.) Finally discuss why it is important to conserve paper and other tree products even though trees are a renewable resource. (Planting trees and harvesting trees take a lot of money and resources. By recycling paper and other tree products, resources such as energy, people's time, and forest land, as well as tree resources, can be saved. Also, if paper consumption continues to climb, more and more land will be needed for pulpwood plantations. And that means less land will be available for native forests and other natural areas. See "Classroom Conservation" in *Project Learning Tree.)*

  Then hold a school-wide or, community-wide paper drive. When the paper is weighed, figure out how many average-sized trees it takes to produce that much paper. (Explain that on the average a 70-foot [21-m] tall tree that is 10 inches [25 cm] in diameter provides about 200 pounds [90 kg] of paper.)

- Use old paper to make new paper (see "Paper in the Classroom" in *Project Learning Tree* or the kits listed under "Booklets, Kits, and Posters" on page 76). You can also recycle cardboard boxes by using them to make crafts.

Hold a "recycled art" contest and have everyone make something from discarded paper products.

- Take a community walk to see where trees grow in your community and what kind of condition they are in. Talk about what the community would be like without any trees. Have someone from the planning or maintenance department in your area talk to your group about how trees are planted, why they are planted where they are, and how people in the community can help care for trees.

- As a group, plant a tree somewhere in the community. Choose a site on the school grounds, in a nature study area, or along a city block. Contact local planning officers or naturalists for advice on where to plant a tree and what type of tree would grow best. Ask if there's a tree planting project that your group could help with. (See "Planting and Caring For Trees" on page 76 for some resources you can use.)

- Raise money for groups that are working to save the world's tropical rain forests. (See "Support Conservation Organizations" on page 55 for more information.)

- Hold an Arbor Day essay contest and have the children write fiction or non-fiction stories about trees. Here are some suggestions for titles:
  —The Planet of the Talking Trees
  —A Day in the Life of Ollie Oak
  —An Interview With Lenny, the Lateral Root
  —The City That Grew Up Around a Tree
  —What a Tree Means to Me

- Have each child come up with an advertising campaign to sell a tree product. To give it a different twist, have each person pretend to be the tree that his or her product comes from. For example, a white ash might advertise baseball bats and a peach tree might advertise peach preserves.

- Have teams of four or five kids research some of the ways trees have influenced our lives through time. Here are some examples of topics they can learn about:
  —the first railroads
  —druids
  —iron smelting during the Iron Age
  —Johnny Appleseed
  —Paul Bunyan
  —shipbuilding

Once they've finished doing research, have each team draw pictures, make collages, or create some other type of display representing their topic. Then have them present what they've learned to the rest of the group.

Picture Poetry

Write picture poems about trees.

Objectives:
Describe what picture poetry is. Write a picture poem about trees.

Ages:
Intermediate and Advanced

Materials:
- **chalkboard or easel paper**
- **drawing paper**
- **pencils**
- **crayons or markers**

Subject:
Poetry

Trees are terrific subjects for poems. And picture poetry is especially fun for kids to write because the poem's words form a picture of what the poem is about.

Before you get started, copy the picture poem below onto a chalkboard or large piece of easel paper. Then ask the kids if they can think of words that describe trees. (List the words they come up with in a place where everyone can see them.) The list might include the words *towering, huge, musty, mossy, slippery, gnarled, twisted, knobby, rough, bumpy, smooth, witchlike, dead, skinny,* and so on. (You might want to take the kids outside and let them look at several trees and feel their bark before you brainstorm a list of adjectives.)

Now tell the kids that when we hear or read descriptive words that make pictures in our minds, we say that the words are a form of *imagery.* For example, have the kids imagine "an old tree by the side of a road." Ask them what they imagined. Then have the kids try to picture "a gnarled tree whose long branches bend over a road like huge arms." Ask them how the second tree they imagined was different from the first. Explain that the second sentence created a more precise image because it described the tree in more detail and used more descriptive words.

Next explain that words can also be written so that they form a picture right on the page itself. Then point to the picture poem you copied. Ask the kids if the poem would be as much fun to read if it were just written across the page instead of in the form of a picture. Talk about how some of the words (for example, *flutter, float,* and *drift)* are written in a way that describes their meaning.

Now have the group make up their own tree picture poems. Be sure to explain that the words in their poems can rhyme if they want them to but that they don't have to rhyme. Also, the lines don't have to be a certain length, and punctuation isn't necessary. The kids just have to form a picture with the words that they write.

THERE'S A HUGE OAK IN MY YARD

LEAVES FLUTTER FLOAT DRIFT DOWN TO THE GROUND

AND I HAVE TO RAKE THEM INTO A PILE

COPYCAT PAGE

FROM PAPER TO PLASTIC

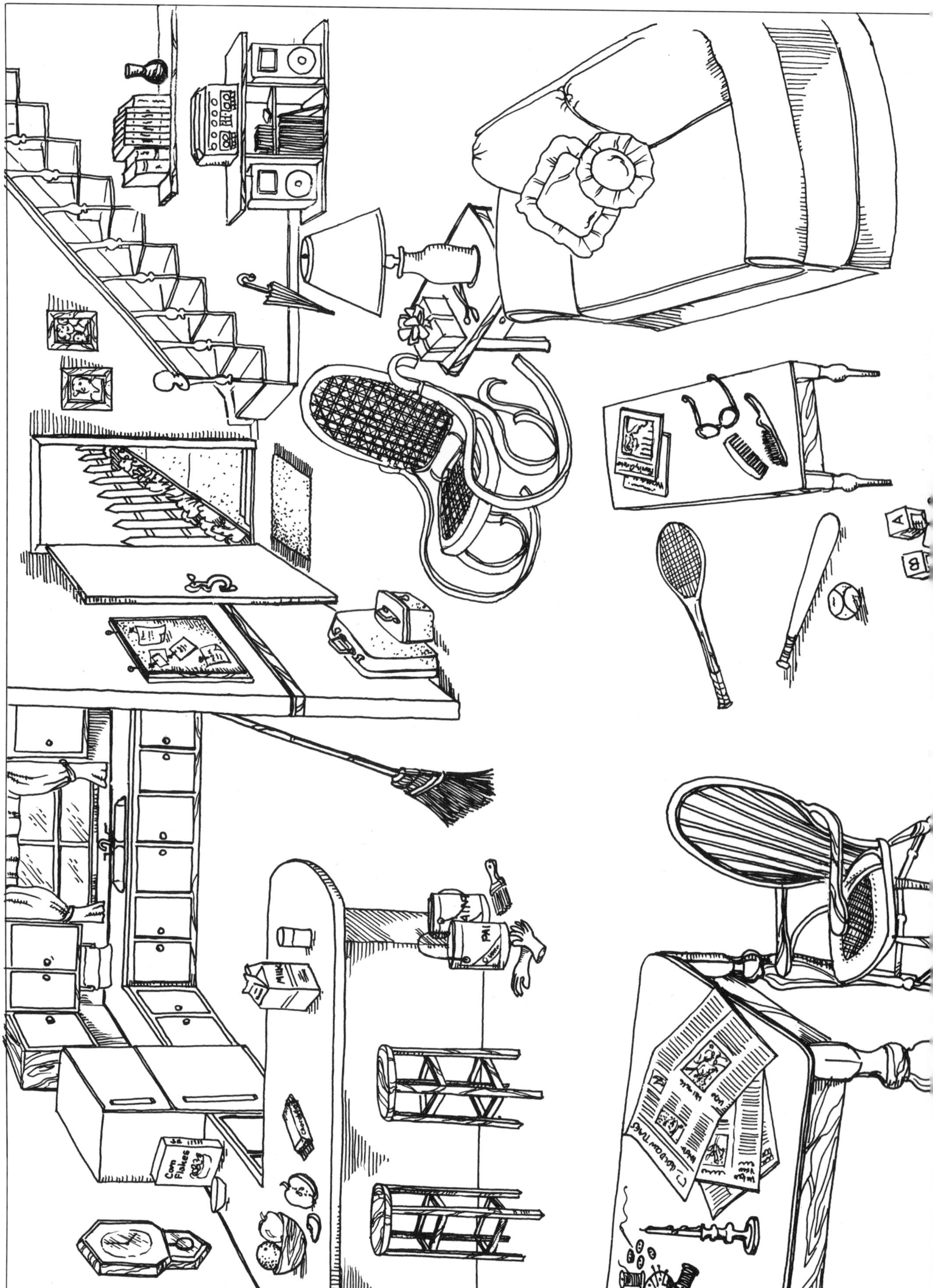

CRAFTY CORNER

Here are some tree art and craft ideas you can use to complement many of the activities in the first five sections.

3-D Trees

Make a three-dimensional picture that shows some of a tree's basic parts.

Ages:
Primary

Materials:
- *construction paper*
- *large pieces of white paper (each at least 11 × 25" [28 × 63 cm])*
- *scissors*
- *markers or crayons*
- *yarn*
- *glue*
- *empty toilet paper rolls*

Subject:
Arts and Crafts

Your kids can have fun making their own three-dimensional trees. Here's how to make one:

1. To make the tree's trunk, cut a toilet paper roll in half lengthwise (see diagram 1). Be sure to cut it so that both halves are the same size.
2. Using markers or crayons, color in bark and knotholes on both halves.
3. Tape the halves end-to-end in the center of a large piece of white paper. Be sure to leave plenty of space above the trunk for the leafy crown and beneath the trunk for the roots (see diagram 2).
4. To make the leaves, cut out small triangles from colored construction paper. Fold each triangle in half, put glue on one of the halves, and stick it to the paper.
5. To make the tree's roots, cut yarn into different lengths and glue the pieces under the trunk, spreading them out like branching roots (see diagram 3).
6. Finish the picture by drawing in grass, background scenery, and a creature that might live in or near the tree.

These 3-D trees are great for using in a discussion about the different parts of a tree. (For information on roots, trunk, bark, and leaves, see pages 6–7.)

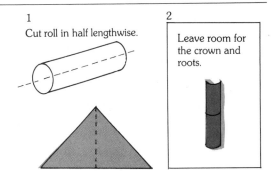

1 Cut roll in half lengthwise.

2 Leave room for the crown and roots.

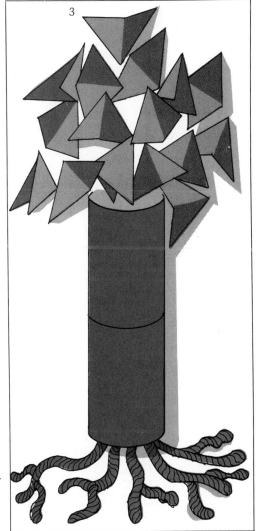

3

Glue on yarn for roots.

Tree Creatures

Make animals out of tree parts.

Ages:
Primary and Intermediate

Materials:
- *Brazil nuts*
- *construction paper*
- *felt-tipped markers*
- *scissors*
- *glue*
- *modeling clay*
- *plastic pantyhose eggs*
- *dried pine needles*
- *acorns*
- *pine scales from pine cones*
- *dried pine tree twigs (with needles attached)*

Subject:
Arts and Crafts

You can use tree parts to make all kinds of "crafty" creatures. Here are a couple of ideas.

THE NUTTY BUNCH

Follow these easy steps to turn Brazil nuts into tiny beavers, penguins, and mice:

1. Draw and cut out animal heads, feet, tails, and other parts (see patterns).
2. Dab a bit of white glue on the pattern pieces and place them on the nuts as shown in the drawings of the different animals. (To curl the mouse's tail, wrap the tail piece tightly around a pencil.)
3. For the beaver and mouse, draw eyes on the nuts with a felt-tipped marker.
4. If an animal won't stand up on its own, make a stand out of modeling clay and press the nut into it.

A PORCUPINE PAL

Luise Woelflein

Here's how to make a prickly porcupine:

1. Work a thin layer of brown modeling clay over the entire surface of a plastic pantyhose egg. (The more you work with the clay the softer it will become, making it easier to add pine needles for quills later.)
2. To make the porcupine's face, glue on acorns for the eyes, a pine cone scale for the nose, and a twig for the mouth.
3. Add clay or acorn-cap feet (see illustration).
4. Insert dried pine needle quills into the clay along the porcupine's back and sides, starting at one end and working your way to the other end.
5. To give your porcupine a tail, first form a small ball of clay. Insert a dried pine twig that has a bunch of needles on it into the ball, then press the ball onto the porcupine.

APPENDIX
Questions, Questions, and More Questions

1. True or false: Trees are considered to be annuals. (False. Annuals are plants that sprout, reproduce, and die in one season. Trees, though, are a type of perennial, which means they live for many seasons.)
2. True or false: Gymnosperms do not produce true flowers or fruit. (True)
3. Name a kind of tree that's a gymnosperm. (Spruces, firs, pines, hemlocks, redwoods, and other conifers are all gymnosperms.)
4. What are deciduous trees? (trees that lose their leaves each year)
5. A tree's outer covering, or _____, protects it from injury, insect damage, and disease. (bark)
6. The sapwood carries _____ and _____ from the roots to the leaves. (nutrients, water)
7. True or false: Pine needles are leaves. (True)
8. What gives green plants their green color? (a pigment called chlorophyll)
9. Name five products people get from trees. (lumber, paper, food, spices, rubber, cork, drugs, fabric—for more examples see pages 65 and 66)
10. The science of managing forests is called _____. (forestry)
11. List three plant layers found in many forests. (canopy, understory, shrub, herb, forest floor, tree trunk, emergent)
12. True or false: Many wild animals spend most of their time in only one or two layers of a forest. (True).
13. True or false: Evergreen trees never shed their leaves. (False. Most evergreen trees gradually replace their leaves, shedding some every year.)
14. Name one function of a tree's trunk. (support rod, transport system)
15. True or false: Broad-leaved trees are also called softwoods. (False. Broad-leaved trees are also called hardwoods. Needle-leaved trees are called softwoods.)
16. Some scientists have divided the world's forests into four major groups. What are they? (boreal, mixed, deciduous, tropical)
17. What is a compound leaf? (a leaf made up of many leaflets)
18. True or false: All broad-leaved trees are deciduous. (False. Some broad-leaved trees are evergreens and do not drop all their leaves each year.)
19. In which leaf layer are stomata found? (epidermis)
20. What two layers make up a leaf's mesophyll? (spongy, palisade)
21. Why do many deciduous trees' leaves change from green to other colors in fall? (In fall chlorophyll breaks down and other pigments in the leaves become visible.)
22. What are coppiced trees? (trees that grow from the stumps of felled trees)
23. What is a decomposer? (an organism that helps break down dead tissue and turns it into soil)
24. What are pulpwood trees? (trees that will one day be made into paper)
25. The inner bark, or _____, transports water, sugar, and dissolved nutrients to all parts of a tree. (phloem)
26. Name two ways animals use trees. (for food, shelter, nesting sites)

Glossary

Luise Woelflein

angiosperms —flowering plants. The seeds of angiosperms are enclosed in flowers, and later, fruit. Roses, peas, and all broad-leaved trees are angiosperms.

annuals —plants that sprout, reproduce, and die in one season. Tomatoes, daisies, and peas are examples of annuals.

biennials —plants that sprout, reproduce, and die in two seasons. Carrots, turnips, and beets are examples of biennials.

biological control —a natural means of controlling pests.

broad-leaved trees —trees that have broad, flat leaves. Maples, palms, and oaks are examples of broad-leaved trees.

bud —part of a twig that contains growing material for the next season.

cambium —thin layer of cells next to the phloem that makes the trunk, branches, and roots of a tree grow thicker.

canopy —uppermost layer of most forests. The branches and leaves of the tallest trees form the canopy.

chlorophyll —green plant pigment that absorbs the sunlight needed for photosynthesis.

conifers —trees whose seeds develop inside cones. A forest made up of conifers is called a *coniferous* forest.

deciduous trees —trees that lose all of their leaves each year. In temperate regions deciduous trees usually lose their leaves in fall. Maples, ashes, and dogwoods are examples of deciduous trees.

deforestation —the process of clearing forests.

dendrology —the study of trees. A *dendrologist* is a scientist who studies trees.

evergreen trees —trees that do not lose all of their leaves each year. Pines, spruces, and firs are examples of evergreens.

forestry —the science of managing forests.

gymnosperms —plants with seeds that aren't enclosed in flowers or fruit. Conifers are the most common type of gymnosperm.

hardwoods —broad-leaved trees. Most, but not all, hardwoods have harder wood than needle-leaved trees.

heartwood —sapwood that has become filled with resinlike material and no longer transports water and minerals. Also called *old xylem*.

multiple use management —the practice of managing a forest for several different uses (mining, camping, logging, and so on) at one time.

needle-leaved trees —trees with needlelike leaves. Pines, spruces, and redwoods are examples of needle-leaved trees.

perennials —plants that live for many seasons. All trees are perennials.

phloem —pipeline of cells that transports sugar and nutrients to all parts of a tree. Sometimes called *inner bark*.

photosynthesis —the process by which plants use the sun's energy to convert carbon dioxide and water into sugar.

root hairs —very thin, hairlike extensions of a root. Root hairs soak up most of the water and dissolved minerals needed by a tree.

sapwood —the most recently formed layer of wood. Sapwood is made of thick-walled cells that transport water and minerals. Also called *new xylem*.

softwoods —needle-leaved trees. Most, but not all, softwoods have softer wood than broad-leaved trees.

stomata —small pores in a tree's leaves and stems that open to absorb carbon dioxide and release oxygen.

transpiration —the process by which a tree loses water through stomata on its leaves and stems.

xylem —conducting cells in a tree that carry water and minerals to the trunk, branches, and leaves.

1998 UPDATE

TABLE OF CONTENTS

COMMUNITY FORESTRY

When people think of forests, they often think of vast wildernesses of trees "out there," unbroken by buildings, roads, or any sign of people. To be sure, that is one type of forest, but it's not the only one. Did you ever think that the trees in a city or town, taken all together, are a forest?

Look over a town from a high hill, tall building, or airplane, and see how dominant its trees are and how much land they cover, hiding houses, streets, and yards. Then imagine what the view would be like with no trees. In some places, such as the Midwest where there are few wild woods, these *community forests* are the only forests in a sea of prairies or farmland. *Community forestry* is a management approach that treats the urban forest as a whole, and works to help it thrive, especially in and around areas such as parks and public buildings that everyone can enjoy.

What do community forests do for us? Think of all the benefits we get from the living trees around us. They shade us on a hot day. They shade our houses and offices, too, saving energy on air conditioning. They block the wind that chills us in the winter and muffle the noise of city streets. They make oxygen that we breathe and clean the air of pollution. They control erosion, keeping the soil from washing away into lakes and rivers. They provide homes and food for wildlife such as squirrels and birds. They give us fruit and nuts and beautify our view with pretty flowers in spring, green leaves in summer, and bright red and yellow colors in fall. They even give us places to hang a swing, hammock, or bird feeder. What else can you think of that trees do for us?

What do community forests need from us? It can be a hard life for a tree in a city or town. Trees suffer from the same things we do: disease, crowding, insects, hunger, thirst, injury, and neglect. Think of the trees you see on city streets, growing in a four-foot-square hole in the sidewalk, concrete covering their roots, branches broken off by passersby, and car exhaust filling the air. Trees like this need help!

What can we do for trees? Tree care can mean many things. The best thing is to give each tree what it needs most. It may need pruning, water, or fertilizer. It may need help fighting disease or insects. Small trees might do better if they are moved to a roomier or less polluted spot. The community forest may be helped by thinning out some trees so there's more room for those that are left. There are even types of trees we can plant that resist the effects of pollution and disease.

If we look at a town's trees as a forest, we can make a plan that gives us the big picture of what the forest needs. Many times, the first thing we need to do is see what trees we have, by doing a *forest inventory*. And we can teach others how to care for the trees around their homes. There's a lot we can do to help trees!

ACTIVITY: Ask students to list benefits of trees, one for each letter of the alphabet: Apples, Beauty, Cooling, etc.

(Adapted from Heather Karlson, *Pine Tree State Arboretum Outdoor Education Center Learning Guide,* 1997, Augusta, Maine.)

AMERICA THE BEAUTIFUL

When a town or group wants to do something good for trees, they may not know where to start. They might not know how to plan, plant, or care for their community forest, or they may not have the money to do so.

That's why a federal program called America the Beautiful was created in 1990. Every year, millions of federal dollars are passed on to state forestry departments, who grant money and technical advice to towns and cities, who match them with their own funds or services to develop local tree management and community forestry programs. So when a community sees a need for tree help, it can apply for a small grant from the Urban and Community Forestry Assistance Program. It's a working partnership among all levels of government, for the sake of trees. And the work can be done by just about any group, citizens, or agencies, such as school groups, garden clubs, town governments, and more.

The "assistance" part of the Urban and Community Forestry Assistance Program isn't only money. Professional foresters and arborists provide technical information and conduct workshops about tree selection, planting and care, insects and diseases, conducting inventories, or starting and promoting community forestry programs—even how to apply for grants. The experts can also

---

WHAT KIND OF PROJECTS CAN BE DONE? SUGGESTIONS INCLUDE:

- **Tree inventories:** First, take stock of trees, listing their kinds, locations, and condition. Locate really special, old or giant trees. Look for trees that need help. Inventories might even be limited just to school grounds, for a manageable size project.
- **Plans:** Develop long-range tree management and planting plans for the whole town, or smaller areas such as parks or schools.
- **Safety plans:** Plan what to do if a storm damages trees, and how to remove and replace them. Look for problem trees, such as those that might fall on power lines or roads. Develop fire management plans in forested communities.
- **Planting and tree care:** Plant trees! The federal program has a goal of planting and maintaining almost a billion trees A YEAR nationwide. Reforest areas that have lost trees. Provide tree care, too:

Watering, weeding and fertilizing are some of the activities anyone can do, and grants can help buy materials.
- **Trails:** Build self-guided forest nature trails, for educating kids and adults about trees and forest ecology.
- **Arboreta and outdoor classrooms:** Create a community arboretum, a park where trees of many kinds can be planted and used as a demonstration site, living laboratory, and educational area, as well as being beautiful.
- **Public awareness and education programs:** Teach others in the community how important trees are and how to care for them. Develop environmental awareness programs to promote benefits of trees and proper tree care in school curricula. Train high schoolers to teach younger kids. Develop displays, materials, or audiovisuals to help teach about the subject.

connect towns and organizations to other sources of information, funds, o seedlings. There's lots of help available out there for people who want to ge involved helping trees.

Other sources of information and/or seedlings:

- National Arbor Day Foundation
  100 Arbor Ave.
  Nebraska City, NE 68410
  (402) 474-5655
  Web page: www.arborday.org
- National Tree Trust
  1120 G St., NW, Suite 770
  Washington, DC 20005
  (202) 628-8733

- American Forests
  1516 P St., NW
  Washington, DC 20005
  (202) 667-3300
  Web page: www.amfor.org

WILDLIFE TREES AT SCHOOL

Schoolyards are gaining wide recognition as terrific places to learn about an enhance nature. Creating wildlife habitat projects, outdoor classrooms, and gai dens in schoolyards has become a valuable as well as convenient way to cor nect students to the outdoors, and benefit the local environment. Whethe you're working from an urban lot, lawn-covered suburban grounds, or ope rural landscape, there's an endless number of projects you can do to bring tree and wildlife habitat to your school's surroundings, while creating good "hab tats" for learning as well. Here's one example, from a teacher at Barnett Shoa Elementary School in Athens, Georgia.

REFORESTATION Our school site was literally treeless. Using trees availabl from the city and local nurserymen, students planted a 15-acre arboretum tha includes oaks, dogwoods, sweetgum and other trees. Now, four years later, th trees are 10 to 15 or more feet tall. Students observe them as the season change and as more and more birds use them for a home. Trees were plante by our earth shelter to provide shade and conserve energy, and also by th parking lot for shade and aesthetic value.

A Native Flora Garden has just been completed. It is divided into three area Wetland, Granite Outcrop, and Upland Forest. Trees and plants indigenous t each area have been planted. We planted endangered pitcher plant seeds in ou grow lab and transplanted them into the bog last spring. Students are studyin these plants, their needs, history, and use.

One school staff parking area looked like a barren desert—no trees, just dry grass. Sawtooth oaks were planted in a row defining the area and shading it. The trees separate the ballfield and the parking area, and provide nesting places for many birds as well.

Joan Goul

This grand old holly tree whose roots were exposed by careless digging was rescued by building up the soil around it. The additional soil also provided a bed for our new herb garden. The tree in the background gives an esthetically pleasing setting for the garden as well as a favorite place for students to sit, read, and observe and smell the herbs.

Joan Gould

RECLAMATION A 100-year-old holly tree, whose roots had been scraped partially bare by bulldozers making room for extra classroom trailers, was reclaimed when the trailers left. The area was terraced and additional soil was added, and it is now a lovely herb garden. Herbs are raised and planted each spring by students and are used for herbal vinegars, dried herbs, and decorations which are sold at an annual holiday sale.

HABITATS A butterfly garden was designed in the shape of a butterfly wing to beautify our entrance as well as to encourage the presence of and provide food for butterflies. Host plants for larva and food plants for adult butterflies were planted. Students did the planting and built a brick walkway meandering through the garden. It is here, as well as in the herb garden, where we find eggs that we hatch into butterflies. These are taken into the classroom where the students can watch the entire metamorphosis process. When the butterflies hatch, the students release them in the garden. We propagated some milkweed seeds (it does not grow down here, but monarchs do migrate through), and we were able to raise some monarchs from the eggs we found.

Bird habitats have been established to help in natural pest control for our gardens. When we first started the habitats, we saw very few birds. Now we see many birds since we provide food, water, and shelter. Most of the classrooms have window feeders so students can see birds up close. Bluebirds were becoming scarce, so we made several bluebird boxes and put them up around school. Now each year we have many families of bluebirds. A class made thirty boxes and made a bluebird trail on a neighbor's fence line. In addition to these habitats, a purple martin complex was made, and each February or early March the martins migrate back. These and other bird houses are made from gourds raised by the students.

We also built habitat for small animals, by piling yard waste into a brushpile, and making a rockpile. These attract chipmunks, squirrels, and skunks.

To teach about the importance of pollination, we installed two working beehives. The honey is sold at our annual sale. We also have an inside observation hive where students can closely watch the hive activity.

RECYCLING AND SEDIMENT CONTROL Garden waste, grass clippings, and kitchen scraps are all put into the mulch pile. Four worm barrels also help with decomposing kitchen waste from our cafeteria. All this wonderful rich soil is then used in our gardens.

An old playground site located on an incline is in the process of being reclaimed thereby controlling erosion. The school, neighborhood, businesses, and Partners In Education are working together to collect #2 plastics to help defray the cost of plastic wood for terracing. Each grade will raise vegetables there in our Giving Garden and give them to the Homeless Shelter and the Food Bank in Athens. This is an effort to encourage recycling and also to recognize and respond to the needs of our community.

These are some of the things that we have done at our school. We can always think of something else to do to enhance and help our environment, and at the same time teach our children their responsibility to planet Earth, now and in the future.

Schoolyard Habitats is a project of the National Wildlife Federation's highly successful Backyard Wildlife Habitat program. Since 1973, NWF has certified over 20,000 wildlife habitats located in homeowners' backyards, common community areas, places of worship, and schools. Over the years, school communities have grown increasingly interested in schoolyard wildlife habitat projects as they allow their students a means to learn and understand their local environment; apply concepts learned in the classroom to tangible, real-life situations; connect with the local community; and take positive action on an issue, habitat conservation, in their own communities.

To learn more about the Schoolyard Habitats project, check out our website at http://www.nwf.org/habitats. For a Schoolyard Habitats Information Kit, please call 410-516-6583. Included in the Kit is a planning guide (complete with example habitat plans/landscape drawings) and a PRE-PAID application for certification. Once the school is certified, it automatically receives a subscription to the quarterly "Habitats" newsletter, a poster, and notices of special events such as International School Grounds Day.

DISEASE BUSTERS—NO MORE NIGHTMARES ON ELM STREET

One reason that trees die is from disease. It can be a real problem for community forests. The American elm tree is a prime example. Millions of elms once grew to giant size all along the streets of American cities and towns. For 300 years of our history, they were one of our favorite street trees and the most planted tree in the U.S.

Then, in the 1930s, disaster struck. Dutch elm disease was accidentally imported from Europe in elm logs. The disease is a fungus carried by tiny bark beetles. The fungus travels through the tree's vascular system and eventually chokes it. The disease killed over half of the elms by 1950, and by now has wiped out over 100 million trees. Streets that once were cool and shady were suddenly hot and bare. It looked like the elm was doomed.

How could this species be saved? Researchers began work to discover ways to treat the disease, and learned to prune the trees and inject fungicide into the trunks every year. To replace lost trees, they located elms that resisted Dutch elm disease, and protected and grew more of these trees that didn't get sick. Over fifty years and many tree generations, with this careful selection and breeding process, they eventually developed the American Liberty elm. This tree survives by walling off the fungus and keeping it from spreading inside the tree. It also tolerates pollution, salt, drought, heat and cold, so it can live in many places. Since 1983, over a quarter million of these trees have been planted in over 750 communities nationwide, and some are now 30 to 40 feet tall.

The Elm Research Institute, or ERI, a nonprofit group in New Hampshire, funded this research, and now grows and distributes American Liberty elm seedlings. ERI has a goal of planting 1 million of these special trees. They have help from groups all across the U.S. that plant the young trees, or raise seedlings and sell them. Student groups, neighborhood associations, city governments, civic organizations, and others have gotten into the act:

- A second-grade Brownie troop in Fairfield, Connecticut saved enough recyclable bottles to buy and plant a Liberty elm at a historic homestead.
- Third graders at Yarmouth Elementary School in Maine got 100 seedlings from ERI and planted them in the town nursery. The seedlings, when a couple of years older, will be transplanted around town.
- Students at the Martin Luther King Magnet and Pleasant Valley Elementary Schools in Schenectady, New York, celebrated Earth Day by helping plant fifty young elms in a nursery at a nature preserve.
- Some youth groups, including many Boy Scout troops, get into the project big-time. With seedlings donated by ERI, they start their own nurseries, care for tiny seedlings for two or three years till they get big enough to transplant to permanent locations, then sell them as a fundraising project. They've started over 650 nurseries this way. Often they find help from local businesses or civic groups who sponsor their efforts— a real "community" forestry effort.

Caring for the seedlings involves several things. Careful planting, fertilizing, fencing to keep out hungry animals, weeding, watering, staking, pruning, and pest control if needed, are some of the things kids do to take care of their tiny trees till they're big enough to go out in the world.

These special trees can only be obtained from ERI and local groups who raise them, to control the purity of the strain or genetic stock. They make a point of planting the trees in public places, such as town halls, libraries, parks, main streets and historic sites, where everyone can enjoy them. Individuals can sponsor trees to be planted on the street in front of their homes, or receive one seedling of their own if they join ERI.

When you plant a tree, you're doing something that makes a difference long after your own lifetime.

The Elm Research Institute provides information and materials for individuals or organizations who want to care for elms or plant new ones, or to groups to start nurseries. They can be reached on Elm Street (where else!), Westmoreland, NH 03467. Their web address is www.forelms.org.

TREE CLIMBER TO THE MAX

Steve Puleo is a professional *arborist,* or person who takes care of trees. He travels all around southern Maine, inspecting trees and giving them the attention they need. Whether it's pruning, planting, feeding or other activities, from the ground to the highest treetops, an arborist is the expert. Walk with Steve around any area that has trees, and you'll learn how to tell when they need help and how to care for them. Take an average backyard, for instance...

"First, let's see what's here," Steve begins. "There are lots of maples—red, Norway, silver; an American elm; white pines and blue spruce. Over there are some chokecherries, and crabapples there, and pin oaks. Now let's take a closer look and see how healthy they are."

"This young elm is a real treasure, since it seems to be resisting Dutch elm disease," he explains. "But it needs pruning. We want to train it so it will grow up tall, not spread outward down low where it will be in the way. I'd cut back the lowest branches, and favor the tallest upright one—the leader, it's called—so it can grow fastest. Next year we can cut the lowest branches off altogether."

Next he looks at a row of evergreens. "Here's some spruce that look healthy—for now. But see how the branches grow right down to the ground? We have to watch out for *Cytospora* (sy-TOSS-por-uh) canker, a tree disease that grows underneath where there's not much air. We'll cut off the very lowest branches so fresh air can get in."

"Here's some sawfly larvae in the Scotch pines," he says, pointing to some squirmy caterpillars. "They eat the needles. Better spray them with Bt—that's *Bacillus thuringiensis,* a bacterium that only kills caterpillars. It's more natural than most pesticides."

On one of the maple trees, tiny bumps cover the leaves. "Those are galls," Steve explains. "And they're nothing to worry about! They're made by tiny wasps that are beneficial insects, since they're parasites on bugs that damage crops. And these galls don't harm the tree."

Steve looks out over the yard. "Most of these trees were planted too deep, and it's keeping them from really growing fast," he points out. "They should have been planted so the soil just covers where the big roots come out from the trunk. But we can fix that! Dig away the soil, level it off, cover the soil with an inch of bark mulch, and we should really see a difference in their growth rate."

"Here's the most common mistake people make with their trees," he says. "This young maple was planted much too close to the house. It'll never have room to grow to full size, and its branches will hit the house. But since it's still small, we can dig it up and move it farther away."

This is the sort of work a professional arborist does daily to keep trees healthy. "It's such a great feeling to keep 'em alive," he says. "You should see the trees I get to work on sometimes. They're the biggest ones around, the real giants." And the work can get really exciting. "When you're dangling from ropes ninety feet up in the top of a salty red oak, trying to trim dead branches, hanging out over a fifty-foot cliff, looking down on rocks and crashing surf—and a strong wind comes up—it's a thrill!"

Arborists are in great demand during and after big storms, too. "We have to remove trees from power lines," he notes. "During Hurricane Gloria, my crew and I (arborists always work in crews of at least two people, for safety) stood on power lines like tightrope walkers, so we could attach ropes to big trees and lift them off the wires. Since we understand the physics of roping, and could use nearby trees to lift the fallen ones, we saved the wires from breaking and needing to be restrung, which would have cost more time and money. Of course," he laughs, "it wasn't that bad—the power company did shut off the electricity while we were wire-walking!"

When asked how he knows so much, it's clear that years of hands-on experience and study of the latest scientific information makes a good arborist. "All professional arborists have two to four years of college in *arboriculture* or forestry," he says. "Arborists need to be able to climb trees, do hard physical work, and use power equipment; but most of all, they need to understand science, especially botany, to be able to tell what individual trees need. We take care of one tree at a time, whether we're responsible for a few in someone's yard or thousands in a city's community forest," he explains. "Oh, and arboriculture is an occupation for both men and women," he adds. "I know of many climbing and consulting arborists that are women."

Communication skills are important, too, he stresses. "A large part of what we do is inform others about the process trees go through to grow. People don't understand that trees change through the year, and that some times are better for tree treatments than others. And that the tree's needs have to come first if they are to survive. We try to encourage a tree-friendly environment!"

Steve also volunteers on community forestry boards; like many arborists, he's a real activist for trees. But he's not alone, especially where kids are concerned. "Many arborists give talks and help plant trees at schools. Or they start an adopt-a-tree program. Kids can locate trees they think need care; every town has trees that are neglected by the owner or town since they are so costly to care for. Then arborists organize and do the needed work, and the students can watch it done on a field trip. Often the kids can even help with cleanup, and they learn a lot about trees. Kids can also encourage establishment of a trust fund or endowment, or raise funds, to care for the trees they adopt."

So you may well find one or more people like Steve in your town. Invite them to teach you how to care for your town's trees!

TREE TALK

Trees can't talk, so how can they tell us when they need help? They do have ways to show us, if we know how to look. Then, if we find a problem, what does it mean? And what do we do about it? This chart may help.

WHAT TO LOOK FOR:

Trunk:
- Damage, dent, wound
- Small round holes
- Cracked or split
- Carved initials
- Rotten spot
- Leaning

- Crowded

- Weedy around base

What it says:
- Injury
- Insects
- Lightning or frost
- Vandalism
- Disease or insects
- Too close to building, not enough light, growing on slope, or pushed on by object
- Too close to other trees, leaving too little light and food for all
- Too much competition

Branches:
- Broken or broken off; stubs left

What it says:
- Damage by storms or people (some from old age)

Leaves:
- Light green or yellow in summer
- Edges brown
- Suddenly brown
- Fall-colored too early
- Spots

- Holes
- Bumps
- Rolled, wrinkled, or distorted shape
- Sudden drop

What it says:
- Lack of food

- Dryness, heat, road salt, or damage
- Frost, disease, or injury
- Damage
- Disease, insects, pollution, or fertilizer/pesticide damage
- Insects
- Insects
- Herbicides, insects, disease, or cold
- If only a few, drought; if a lot, disease or boring insects

WHAT TO DO:

Prune—Guides and stimulates growth, cuts off dead or diseased wood

Water—In summer and winter dry spells

Feed with fertilizer—In fall, when trees need food for winter and it won't be lost to the surrounding environment, feed with compost, which is longest-lasting and best for soil. Second choice is a low-nitrogen, slow-release granular type of manmade fertilizer.

Remove insects—Use biological controls like predatory insects, or pesticides if necessary.

Uncover roots covered by pavement, where possible.

Remember, dead trees are worthwhile, too. If the tree is past saving, keep it anyway, and watch its changes as it becomes a wildlife tree.

PEOPLE OF THE FOREST

I like trees. Trees saved my skin last summer.

I came to appreciate trees of the rainforest on a hike in Sumatra, a huge island in the northern part of Indonesia. That's a country on the opposite side of the world from America. I wanted to see what a real, original, primary rainforest was like, and, as a wildlife biologist, I hoped to see what animals live there.

But when I found myself pulling myself up a steep trail by slim tree trunks, and climbing up stairsteps formed by their roots, which were all that held together the slippery yellow mud, I came to appreciate trees as never before. I still remember their smooth bark and willowy strength, and admired how they clung to life on hillsides. The trees seemed to literally hold the hill together. I walked on

Carol J. Boggis

ridgetops so narrow there was barely room for the path, and the ground dropped off sharply on both sides of me. If I slipped, it would be a painfully long slide to the bottom—except that the trees would catch me! I was glad it hadn't rained, or it would have been much too slippery to take my hike. The terrain was so steep that I was often level with the tops of very tall trees growing in the deep valley below—that is, when the thick jungle let me have a view!

The trees were enormous, taller than almost any I'd ever seen, especially the eucalyptus trees (also called resin or gum trees). Many trees propped themselves up with wide wings, or buttresses, angling out from their trunks to the ground. They reminded me of curving dinosaur tails, and were like no trees I'd ever seen at home in the U.S. There were bamboo trees, too, and many other species that had no English names. Many trees had long, thick vine-like plants, called *lianas* (lee-Ah-nuz), attached to them high up in their branches, that hung to the ground in a tangle. Sometimes I used these to pull me up a steep part in the trail. Orchids grew high up the tree trunks. A thin layer of leathery rotting leaves on the jungle floor made the damp forest smell mushroomy and pungent. It was hot, humid, very still, and silent—for awhile.

HOO'S THERE?

Suddenly, I heard a loud hooting off in the trees. My Indonesian guide, a young man named Idris, said, "Hear that? It's a gibbon." Black-throated gibbons, or siamangs, can be heard for miles, calling to each other. But we never saw it. Once we glimpsed some long-tailed macaques (muh KAKS), medium-sized tan monkeys, shyly sitting in a tree far off.

We hiked up and down ridges, across tiny streams, past a trickling little waterfall and mossy green cliffs. Then we heard huge wings rustling and flapping overhead. It was a hornbill, a black bird as big as an eagle with a long, curved yellow beak. The wind swished loudly through its feathers as it flew from treetop to treetop, where it would land to eat the fruit that grew there. Then it cackled, calling with what sounded like crazy laughter.

Michael S. Hamilton

As we hiked along, Idris warned me not to touch the trees that had ants climbing up them—"Some of them bite," he explained. And I could tell that it was smart not to grab the prickly vines of rattan. Some Indonesians actually cut the vines, avoiding the spines, peel them, and bend and weave them into rattan furniture. It's one of many products the local people get from the forest.

ORANGE ORANGUTANS

Suddenly, Idris stopped us and pointed. "Orangutan!" he said. There, in the trees just over our heads, was a big rusty-red ape—a young mother. Her fuzzy little baby clung to her and peeked out at us with bright eyes. "These two come here often," Idris said. "Let's give them one of the bananas we brought." He pulled a greenish banana from his backpack, and the mother orangutan stretched out her long, long arm and hand and took the banana. She peeled it very quickly with her teeth and ate it in one bite. Her baby watched but was too young to like bananas yet.

"Why are they so tame?" I asked.

"Because they're used to people," Idris answered. "The mother orangutan, and others like her, were once captured illegally from the forest and kept in captivity as pets. The government found them, and brought them near here to the Bohorok Orangutan Rehabilitation Center, who trained them to survive on their own again in the forest. Mostly, that is," he laughed, as he gave out another banana.

"Don't they get spoiled by eating free bananas, and not learn to find their own food?" I asked.

"Bananas aren't their favorite food," he said. "So when they're being trained to go back to the forest, they only get bananas and milk. Pretty soon, they find fruit that they like better, like figs from the forest trees, and don't come back for bananas any more."

I reached out my hand, and the orangutan gently took it in her own. Her palm was cool, smooth and soft like fine leather. The red-brown fur on her arm was thin, but soft and clean. She looked at me peacefully, then moved away through the branches.

"Wow," I breathed. "I just held hands with an endangered species!"

Carol J. Boggis

TREES IN TROUBLE

Seeing them, it was clear to me how much orangutans depend on forests. They use them for food and shelter, make nests in the trees every night, and cover themselves with leafy branches in rainstorms. They eat many kinds of fruit from trees. They eat insects that live on and inside the trees, and use twigs as tools to get at honey stored there by bees. When there's no fruit, they even eat the trees, peeling the bark and chewing the soft layer inside. They're such acrobats, they rarely have to come down to the ground, and so escape enemies like tigers—and people.

Sadly, orangutans are disappearing fast, and not only because people catch them. The rainforests where they live are being cut down, the giant trees logged for plywood, and the land changed to agriculture such as rice paddies. Fires burn the forests, too, to make way for plantations of oil palm trees, rubber trees, and bananas. So the forests are in danger, and along with them the orangutans, butterflies, orchids, leaf monkeys, hornbills, siamangs, and tigers that live there.

Our hike was in an area protected from logging, the Mount Leuser National Park. But just outside the Park's borders, all the native rainforest trees had been cut down for plantations. And people have been pushing on the borders, to cut inside the Park too. Where will the orangutans be reintroduced, if less and less forest is available for them to live in? Out of all the world, only two percent of their original habitat remains, and now orangutans live on only two Indonesian islands. On the other one, Borneo or Kalimantan, another rehabilitation center is now so far from forest, it has to truck the apes a long way to release them.

TREE PEOPLE

"Orangutan" comes from Indonesian words: *Orang* means man or person, *utan* means forest. Where will these "people of the forest" live, if not in their forest? How will the forest be protected?

Indonesians love orangutans as we do— they even show them on their paper money—so they are trying to solve this problem. The government has ordered timber companies to stop clearing the land by fire, at least for now. Environmentalists are fighting for orangutan and forest protection measures. But it's a complex problem, with big companies, struggling small farmers, government officials, and many more involved, each with different interests. It is to be hoped that they can find a way to save room in their forests for orangutans, too.

FORESTS AFIRE!

Forest fires are big news. The fires of 1988 that burned almost a million acres in Yellowstone made America feel its favorite National Park was burning down. Vast areas of rainforest are burned every year by fires set to clear land, such as in Brazil. In Indonesia in 1997, plantation fires escaped during drought and burned out of control, their smoke darkening the skies for hundreds of miles.

Fires are a frightening force that can be very destructive of forests, habitats, property, and lives, especially if they become massive. Large, intense fires also contribute to global warming by emitting enormous amounts of carbon dioxide and methane as byproducts, and by destroying trees that normally absorb greenhouse gases during respiration. And they may cause the extinction of unknown numbers of species, especially in rainforests where biodiversity is so great and species limited in range.

Fires aren't all bad news, however. The first appearance of devastation can be deceptive, and many ecosystems do recover from damage. For example, scientists studying the 1988 Yellowstone fires discovered that only 17 of the Park's moose, bears, deer, and bison died, and only one percent of the 30,000 elk. Though it was feared that many more would starve the following winter, food shortages from the fires caused only six to ten percent more winter deaths than usual. As for plants, though a third of the Park was burned, the fires left a mosaic of burned and unburned patches that allowed rapid reseeding and regrowth. The soil was charred only one inch deep in most places, so roots survived and plants quickly resprouted.

Ecologists have long understood that fire is a natural, even essential part of some forests, especially those that have evolved to depend on fire. They have learned that protecting forests from all fires, as has been done in the past, allows excess leaves, pine needles, dead grass, small trees, and dry brush, called fuels, to build up into fire-prone conditions that set the stage for really big fires that are hard to control.

FRIENDLY FIRE

While unchecked fires are hazardous, people discovered long ago how to control and use fire. They made it a valuable tool for cooking food, keeping warm, and many other purposes. Now forest managers are developing methods of using forest fires as a tool to keep forests healthy. They may allow some lightning-caused fires to burn, within safe limits. They even sometimes set a fire on purpose, called a "prescribed burn."

PRESCRIPTIONS FOR HEALTHY FOREST

It's a strange idea to think that setting a forest afire is good for it! But that's exactly what U.S. forest managers do, when conditions are just right to do so safely in a controlled situation. Why? Setting small fires to imitate natural fires, or letting natural fires burn, removes excess fuels under big trees without destroying all the trees. This kind of surface or ground fire has always burned in California's groves of giant sequoias, and these trees have survived such fires for centuries.

Getting rid of fuel reduces the chance of its building up so much that, if lightning or a careless camper ignites it, it will burn everything in its path in an intensely hot wildfire. That would be like having too much tinder on a campfire, which bursts up into a giant bonfire instead of making a warm, slow-burning, controlled fire, one we'd like for toasting marshmallows. Superhot fires burn forests severely, and plants grow back much more slowly than in areas lightly burned.

FIRE'S BENEFITS

Forest protection is only one reason to set small prescribed fires. Small fires open clearings in dense stands of trees, increasing landscape diversity for a wider variety of wildlife and giving plants that need sunlight a chance to grow. The resulting mixture of ages of trees means the next fire won't burn the entire forest at once.

Fires also encourage the growth of plants that are favorite wildlife foods. They leave behind dead trees, or snags, that provide nesting cavities for woodpeckers, bluebirds, and other creatures. (The chapter on "People and Forests" describes more ways fire benefits forests.) Fires may be used to control problem insects, non-native weeds, disease, or to clear brush from a logged area for planting new trees.

ONLY WHEN SAFE

What conditions make it safe for a prescribed burn? Weather conditions must be cool and not windy. The location must be a safe distance from buildings, people, and valuable resources such as prehistoric ruins. Trees and fuels must have high moisture content and other carefully determined factors apply.

Conditions of high temperatures, extreme drought, wind, and dry fuels are too dangerous. In Brazil, Indonesia, and elsewhere, fires have been used as a tool for centuries to cheaply clear rainforest for agriculture, grazing, and plantations; but they spread to immense size when drought and wind, unusual in the humid tropics, swept the fires out of control in those conditions. The usual monsoon rains were expected to put the fires out, but the rains didn't come. Huge areas of rainforest, not adapted to fire, are destroyed this way, intentionally or otherwise.

Some people oppose the use of prescribed fires to manage U.S. forests. They worry that they will be unsafe, or cause health problems from the smoke, or diminish the view. It is hard to see past the short-term loss to the long-term benefits. And the question of forest fire's contribution to global warming is under study. But overall, managers have recognized the necessity of fire as a natural part of the ecosystem. They plan to prescribe fire for millions of acres a year of America's public lands such as national forests, parks, and grasslands.

FRIEND AND FOE

In short, fire is neither good nor bad, but some of both. Most of all, fire means sudden change in the forest community. As forests regrow after a fire, change goes on, but at a slower pace.

The following story illustrates the cycle of change before, during, and after a fire. Hand out copies of the Copycat Page to the class, then have them look at the pictures as you read the story aloud.

After finishing the story, ask the students some questions. How can managers try to mimic normal fire patterns, without causing big fires (by setting small fires, controlling their area, and putting them out; by burning areas as often as they would burn naturally)? Do you think fires have the same effect in other kinds of forest that aren't adapted to fire, like rainforest? What would be the same (immediate devastation; quick regrowth of grass and low plants)? What would be different (extinction of species; loss of thin soil to erosion during heavy rainfall; some areas may never return to forest because tree seeds sprout too quickly, then die in hot, sun-baked soil)? What about in grasslands or shrublands (regrows to original state sooner, since slow-maturing tall trees are absent)?

FURTHER STUDY

Research how fire affects a particular species of plant or animal, and whether and how fire might be used to benefit that species. See the U.S. Forest Service Fire Effects Information Center's website at www.fs.fed.us/database/feis for more information.

For a detailed poster about Yellowstone's fires called "Wildland Fire in the Northern Rockies" and other materials, write the Education Programs Coordinator, National Park Service, P.O. Box 168, Yellowstone National Park, WY 82190. Their website is at www.nps.gov.

THE FOREST THAT LIVES WITH FIRE

Picture A

In the northwest corner of Wyoming lies Yellowstone National Park. It's a huge area of rolling hills covered with forests of lodgepole pines, sparkling trout-filled rivers, vast lakes, grassy meadows, and aspen groves. Stranger sights are here, too: geysers shooting steam high into the air; bubbling mud volcanoes; hot aqua-blue pools whose edges are crusted white and yellow with minerals; cliffs of glassy black obsidian rock; forests of petrified trees; and deep canyons with glorious thundering waterfalls.

Wildlife fills Yellowstone. Herds of elk, bison, moose, pronghorn, and bighorn sheep roam its valleys. Even grizzly bears, mountain lions, and wolves make the great wilderness their home. Many smaller mammals live here, too, from coyotes and badgers right down to snowshoe hares and mice. The forests are musical with the songs of birds, and osprey, eagles, swans, and geese visit the waters. Butterflies sip from meadow flowers, and dragonflies perch on marsh grasses. So it has been in Yellowstone for thousands of years.

Picture B

Occasionally, too, as in many similar forests, fire is a visitor, started by lightning or people. The fire races through the trees and creeps along the ground, crackling through dried grass and dead branches. The air gets very hot and smoky. Large animals such as mule deer and black bears run away, as do smaller ones like rabbits and foxes. Birds fly away from the fire; beavers and other animals that live in water are safe where they are. Chipmunks and insects hide in their burrows below the hot surface. Few animals die, and those that do become food later for scavengers like bears, coyotes, and ravens. The fire burns out when it runs out of forest at a stream or cliff, or when it rains, or where firefighters put it out.

After the fire, the ground is ash-covered and black in patches. Burned tree stumps stick up or lay where they have fallen. When it rains, streams run muddy with dirt and ash. All looks dead.

Picture C

But it doesn't take long for life to come back. Mice and ground squirrels hiding in their burrows come out right away, to eat millions of pine seeds dropped in the fire, and hawks and owls come to catch them. Insects feed or lay eggs on burned trees, and they attract birds like woodpeckers.

Plants soon recover, too, starting within days to regrow from their roots, enjoying the new sunlight without trees overhead. Seeds sprout. Lodgepole pines actually depend on fire to grow new trees, because intense heat is needed to open their pine cones and let the seeds out. As plants grow back and hold the soil in place, the streams run clear again.

Within three years, the ground is thick with green grass, growing fast in the ash-enriched soil. The meadows are colored by wildflowers of pink fireweed and blue lupine. Soft little seedlings of lodgepole pine appear. Aspen tree roots have put up shoots that are leafing out. Bluebirds nest in holes in the burned tree stumps. Bison and elk come to graze on thick grass.

Picture D

In 25 years, a new young forest has grown. Aspen trees shimmer in the breeze, and elk eat their bark in winter. Ten times as many kinds of plants grow here as when it was a shady pine forest. Pine saplings push their way up through the aspen. Someday, in a century or so, they will grow tallest and become dominant.

Picture A again

And the forest will look like it did in the beginning once again, completing the cycle of life in the Forest that Lives with Fire.

SAFETY MESSAGE: Fire has a natural place in many forests, if caused by lightning or by experts who control them. But Smokey the Bear was right in one sense—we should never accidentally cause fires. Never start a fire on purpose, either in nature or at home, unless it is carefully controlled in a fireplace, under the supervision of an adult.

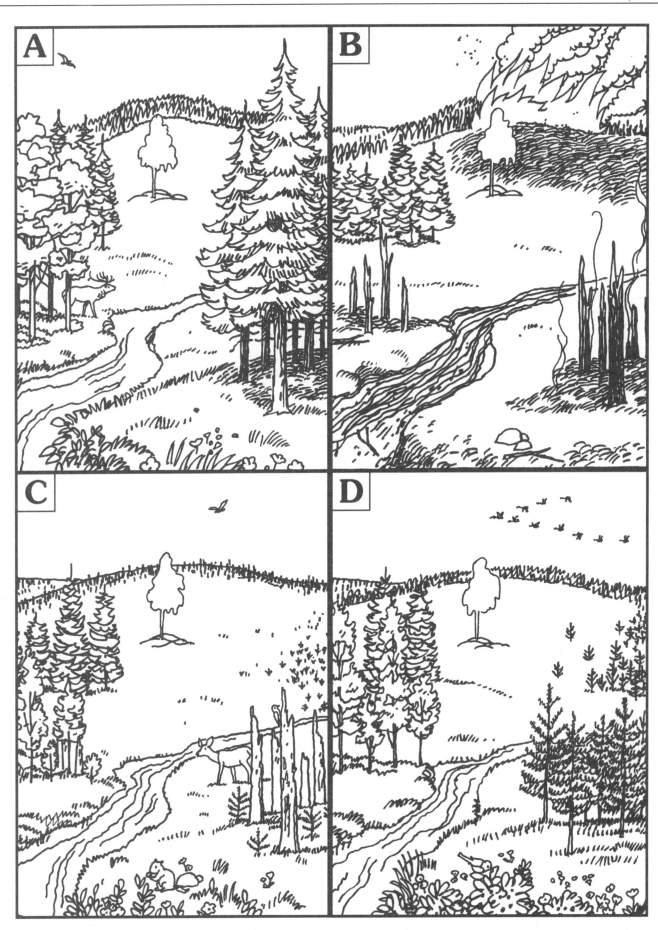

Bibliography

(Note: A * at the end of a listing indicates that a book is a good source of tree pictures.)

GENERAL REFERENCE BOOKS

The Natural History of Trees of Eastern and Central North America by Donald Culross Peattie (Houghton Mifflin, 1991)
A Natural History of Western Trees by Donald Culross Peattie (Houghton Mifflin, 1991)
Tree by David Burnie (Knopf, 1988).*

FIELD GUIDES

Field Guide to Trees and Shrubs by George A. Petrides (Houghton Mifflin, 1973)*
Forest Trees of the United States and Canada and How to Identify Them by Elbert L. Little, Jr. (Dover Publications, 1980)*
National Audubon Society Field Guide to North American Trees, Eastern Region and Western Region (Knopf, 1996)*
Manual of the Trees, 2 vols., by Charles Sprague Sargent (Dover, 1965)*
Trees is a Nature Finder identification wheel. By turning the wheel, information about different trees is displayed through windows. Available from Hubbard Scientific. 1-800-446-8767.
Trees of North America by C. Frank Brockman (Golden Press, 1979)*
The Winter Tree Finder by May Theilgaard Watts (Nature Study Guild, 1970)*

CHILDREN'S BOOKS

Be a Friend to Trees by Patricia Lauber (HarperCollins, 1994). Primary
The Blossom on the Bough by Anne Ophelia Dowden (Tricknor & Fields, 1994). Advanced
The Fall of Freddie the Leaf by Leo Buscaglia, Ph.D. (Charles B. Slack, 1982). All ages
Dead Log Alive! by Jo S. Kittinger (Watts, 1996). Advanced
Exploring Tree Habitats by Patti Seifert (Mondo Publishing, 1994). Primary
A Gift of a Tree is a book with a tree starter seed kit by Greg Henry Quinn (Scholastic, 1994). Primary
The Giving Tree by Shel Silverstein (Harper & Row, 1964). All ages
Have You Seen Trees? by Joanne Oppenheim (Scholastic, Inc., 1995). Primary
How Leaves Change by Sylvia Johnson (Lerner Publications, 1986). Advanced
In the Woods: Who's Been Here by Lindsay Barrett George (Greenwillow, 1995). Primary
Life on a Limb is a pop-up book by Donald M. Silver (W.H. Freeman, 1994).
The Lorax by Dr. Seuss (Random House, 1971). All ages
The Man Who Planted Trees by Jean Giono (Chelsea Green, 1985). Advanced
Outside and Inside Trees by Sandra Markle (Bradberry Press, 1993). Primary*
Pearl Plants a Tree by Jane Breskin Zalben (Simon & Schuster, 1995). Primary
Sky Tree: Seeing Science Through Art by Thomas Locker with Candice Christiansen (HarperCollins, 1995). Primary and Intermediate*
Start Exploring Forests is a coloring book by Betina Dudley (Running Press, 1989). Intermediate and Advanced
Tree by David Burnie (Knopf, 1988). Intermediate and Advanced*
The Tree in the Ancient Forest by Carol Reed-Jones (Dawn, 1995). Primary
A Tree is Nice by Janice May Udry (Harper & Row, 1987). Primary
Tree of Life by Barbara Bush (Little, Brown & Co., 1998). Primary
The Tree That Would Not Die by Ellen Levine (Scholastic, 1995). Primary
Trees by Linda Gamlin (Dorling Kindersley, 1993). Intermediate*
Trees by Ruth Thomson (Usborne, 1980). Primary
Trees by Theresa Greenaway (Dorling Kindersley, 1995). Intermediate and Advanced*
Trees (Scholastic, 1995). Primary and Intermediate
Trees and Forests (Scholastic, 1993). Intermediate and Advanced

AUDIOCASSETTES, VIDEOS, AND VIDEODISCS

Bullfrog Films offers several tree videos for sale and rental, including *Our Vanishing Forests* (Advanced), *Replanting the Tree of Life* (Advanced), and *Tickle the Sky* (Advanced). Call 1-800-543-3764 for more information and to order.
Environmental Media offers numerous tree videos for advanced students, including *Forest Stewardships: Youth Education and Outreach, Fall Color of the Eastern Forest,* and *Headwaters Forest.* Call 1-800-368-3382 for information or to order.
Humans in the Forest and **The Natural Forest** are companion videos from The Video Project, 5332 College Ave., Ste. 101, Oakland, CA 94618. Advanced
National Geographic Society offers several tree titles. Videos include: *Ancient Forests* (Advanced); *Let's Explore a Forest* (Intermediate and Advanced); *Old-Growth Forest: An Ecosystem* (Advanced); *Trees for Life* (all ages); and *Wild, Wonderful Animals in the Woods* (Primary and Intermediate). *Rain Forest* is an STV videodisc containing video clips and still photos, along with a teacher's guide for intermediate and advanced students. *A Tree Through the Seasons* is a Wonders of Learning Kit containing student booklets, audiocassette, and teacher's guide with background and activity sheets for primary students. Call 1-800-368-2728 for more information and to order.
When a Tree Falls is a video from Chip Taylor Communications, 15 Spollett Dr., Derry, NH 03038. Intermediate and Advanced

COMPUTER AND ON-LINE RESOURCES

Forest Biomes is a CD-ROM for Macintosh featuring video clips and background information on both coniferous and deciduous forest ecosystems. Queue, 1-800-775-2724. Intermediate and Advanced
Journey North is an Internet-based program that engages students of all ages in a global study of wildlife migration and seasonal change. Student observations are shared with other classrooms over the Internet. Children can also follow the work of scientists who are tracking the phenomena using various technologies. One of the observations is the leafing out of trees to chart the progress of spring. Participation is free; teachers need only sign up. Teachers can also purchase a packet of supplementary materials, including a 30-page teacher's guide and full-color map. For more information, call (612) 476-6470. Or subscribe at the Journey North Web site—www.learner.org/jnorth.
    National Arbor Day Foundation's Web site contains lots of information to download and put to use, including tips on how to celebrate Arbor Day, how to plant a tree, and information about the Foundation's curriculum kits. Go to www.arborday.org to access the site.
    Rain Forest is a National Geographic Society STV interactive videodisc containing video clips and still photos, along with a teacher's guide for intermediate and advanced students. An optional package with this videodisc includes software containing National Geographic magazine and book excerpts and photo-essays. Call 1-800-368-2728 for information and to order.

PAPER MAKING

    "How You Can Make Paper" is a pamphlet available from the American Forest and Paper Association. They also offer "How Paper Came to America," an informational poster. Both publications are free to teachers. Order by calling 1-800-244-3090.
Minnesota Forest Industries offers a papermaking kit that includes directions and supplies for 30 students to each make a sheet of paper. The group also offers free educational materials to teachers. Write to Minnesota Forest Industries, 314 W. Superior St., Ste. 1015, Duluth, MN 55802; (218) 722-5013. You can also access their Web site—www.mintrees.org—and order the kit or other materials.

OTHER ACTIVITY RESOURCES

American Forests offers two guides geared toward advanced students. *Growing Greener Cities and Environmental Education Guide* is a two-volume set containing a manual for urban tree planting and care and an education guide with 13 activities. *World Forests: Striking a Balance Between Conservation and Development* is an 83-page classroom guide containing 20 activities and background material. For more information, write to American Forests, P.O. Box 2000, Washington, DC 20013.
Animal Inns offers educational materials designed to show that dead trees are still full of life. In addition to information packets, T-shirts, brochures, and posters, the group also offers classroom activities for elementary teachers. Write to Animal Inn Products, P.O. Box 5065, Bend, OR 97708-5065.
Forest and **Neighborhood Woods** are Outdoor Biology Instructional Strategies (OBIS) modules containing 7 and 8 activities respectively. Available from Delta Education by calling 1-800-258-1302. Intermediate and Advanced
National Arbor Day Foundation offers numerous resources for teachers. Their *Trees are Terrific!* curriculum kit for fifth grade contains a video, filmstrip and audiocassettes, two posters, tree identification booklets for 35 students, and teacher's guide with reproducible activity sheets. The *Grow Your Own Tree* curriculum for second grade contains two video programs, two posters, seed planting packets for 35 students, and teacher's guide with activity sheets in both English and Spanish. *Discovery Curriculum* contains background, activities, and resources for tree stewardship lessons for advanced students. For information about these and the Foundation's other educational materials, contact the National Arbor Day Foundation at 100 Arbor Ave., Nebraska City, NE 68410 or visit their Web site at www.arborday.org.
National Science Teachers Association (NSTA) offers an 88-page teacher's guide for Primary grades called *Tree Homes*. For more information or to order, call 1-800-722-NSTA.

93

Project Learning Tree (PLT), an award-winning program of the American Forest Foundation with the Council for Environmental Education, provides supplementary environmental education curriculum materials to teachers and other educators working with students in preK through grade 12. By using the forest as a "window" into natural and built environments, PLT covers the total environment: land, air, and water, and is local, national, and global in scope. PLT activity guides are provided to educators when they participate in a PLT workshop. For more information visit their Web site at www.plt.org or contact Project Learning Tree at 1111 19th St., NW, Ste. 780, Washington, DC 20036: (202) 462-2462.

WHERE TO GET MORE INFORMATION

Area forest industries (logging companies, paper mills, etc.)
- County extension offices
- Arboretums and botanical gardens
- Natural history museums
- National, state, and local parks
- Nature centers
- State departments of forestry or agriculture
- University departments of biology, botany, conservation, and forestry

Natural Resources

Ranger Rick, *published by the National Wildlife Federation, is a monthly nature magazine for elementary-age children.*

Ranger Rick® magazine is an excellent source of additional information and activities on trees and many other aspects of nature, outdoor adventure, and the environment. This 48-page award-winning monthly publication of the National Wildlife Federa-tion is packed with the highest-quality color photos, illustrations, and both fiction and nonfiction articles. All factual information in *Ranger Rick* has been checked for accuracy by experts in the field. The articles, games, puzzles, photo-stories, crafts, and other features inform as well as entertain and can easily be adapted for classroom use. To order or for more information, call 1-800-588-1650.

The EarthSavers Club provides an excellent opportunity for you and your students to join thousands of others across the country in helping to improve our environment. Sponsored by Target Stores and the National Wildlife Federation, this program provides children aged 6 to 14 and their adult leaders with free copies of the award-winning *EarthSavers* newspaper and *Activity Guide* four times during the school year, along with a leader's handbook, EarthSavers Club certificate, and membership cards. For more information on how to join, call 1-703-790-4535 or write to EarthSavers; National Wildlife Federation; 8925 Leesburg Pike; Vienna, VA 22184.

ANSWERS TO COPYCAT PAGES

KEYING OUT TREES (p.22)
1. silver maple
2. horse chestnut
3. black walnut
4. white oak
5. weeping willow
6. white pine
7. Sitka spruce
8. choke cherry
9. honey locust

TREES AROUND THE WORLD (p.33)
1. bristlecone pine, California
2. baobab tree, Africa
3. bald cypress, Louisiana
4. banyan tree, India
5. saguaro cactus, Arizona
6. monkey puzzle tree, Chile
7. ginkgo tree, China
8. eucalyptus or giant gum, Australia
9. cork oak tree, Spain

A WALK IN THE WOODS (p.45)
Douglas squirrel—fir cone; goshawk—nest; banana slug—mushroom; porcupine—bark; hairy woodpecker—beetle grub